How to STOP BULLYING and SOCIAL AGGRESSION

How to STOP BULLYING and SOCIAL AGGRESSION

STEVE BREAKSTONE

MICHAEL DREIBLATT

KAREN DREIBLATT

Elementary Grade Lessons and Activities That Teach Empathy, Friendship, and Respect

Skyhorse Publishing

10 9 8 7 6 5 4 3 2 1

Library of Congress Cataloging-in-Publication Data is available on file.

ISBN: 978-1-62087-218-5

Printed in China

Contents

Acknowledgments

We would like to thank the following people for their assistance in helping us create this book:

Jessica Allan, our editor, for her professionalism and expertise; Joanna Coelho, our editorial assistant, for her professionalism and for always cheerfully answering our many questions; Stacy Wagner, for believing in our project and signing us on with Corwin Press; Doris Bass, whose advice in pitching a proposal was invaluable; Jonah Spivak and Carrie O'Neil at Spectrum Design, for their talent, friendship, and ability to take our amorphous thoughts and turn them into eye-catching design; Jane Glesne, Janet Phipps, Jim Quattrocchi, and Pat Gibbons, for their friendship, support, insights, patience, and willingness to read endless drafts of this book; our good-natured guinea pigs Tyler Dreiblatt, Eric Dreiblatt, and Kevin Kirk who offered their insights and suggestions regarding what works for kids and what doesn't; and, finally, the thousands of students we've worked with over the years—you've taught us so much.

Corwin Press gratefully acknowledges the following peer reviewers for their editorial insight and guidance:

Melissa Albright
Sixth-Grade Teacher
Wilson's Creek 5/6 School
Springfield Public Schools
Springfield, MO

Erin Barrie
School Psychologist
Regional School District #17
Haddam-Killingworth, CT

Sheila Fisher
Principal
Maria Weston Chapman Middle School
Weymouth, MA

About the Authors

 **Steve Breakstone**, cofounder of Balance Educational Services, LLC, is a specialist in student discipline, bullying and violence prevention, behavior management, and effective communication styles. During his dynamic workshops, he uses his theatrical experience to role-play serious realities such as being bullied, being the subject of rumors, or being shunned by cliques. Steve is an expert in the Individuals with Disabilities Education Improvement Act (IDEA 2004) and Section 504 of the Rehabilitation Act, offering easy-to-understand seminars to teachers, administrators, and attorneys.

Steve has served as the Director of Northstar Community Alliance where he worked to prevent and reduce substance abuse. He has also worked to prevent domestic abuse as the Youth and Community Educator with Project Against Violent Encounters. Steve is a past facilitator with FATHERTIME, a parenting program, and is a trained mediator.

In the late 1980s, Steve and his dog, Dixie, walked 3,000 miles from New Orleans to Washington state. In Washington, Steve worked nine years with people with developmental disabilities. He is the author of the book *Washington WALKABOUT*. This book examines the experiences of Reggie Feckley, a man with developmental disabilities as he, Steve, and Dixie walked 1,300 miles around the state of Washington, promoting the capabilities of people with disabilities. Steve lives on thirty acres in Vermont with nature photographer Jane Glesne and their cat.

 **Michael Dreiblatt**, cofounder of Balance Educational Services, LLC, is an outstanding national speaker who concentrates in bullying and violence prevention, creating healthy relationships, and discipline of children with special needs. With his humorous style and engaging stories, he has taught these topics to thousands of adults and students. Michael is an expert in Section 504 of the Rehabilitation Act, the Individuals with Disabilities Education Improvement Act (IDEA 2004), and the No Child Left Behind Act of 2001.

Michael is a former teacher, having taught in New York City and Vermont. He is the past Director of Education for Israel Congregation of Manchester and the former Network Coordinator of the Vermont School Age Care Network, where he advocated for improved after-school programs. He is a past facilitator with FATHERTIME, combining adult/child recreation and the teaching of practical fathering skills. Michael is also an experienced grant writer and trained mediator.

Born and raised in Brooklyn, New York, Michael lives in Manchester Center, Vermont, with his wife, Karen, their two sons, and their dog and cat.

 **Karen Dreiblatt,** cofounder of Balance Educational Services, LLC, has devoted her adult life to bettering the lives of children and claims motherhood as her most fulfilling career choice. Using her background in psychology, Karen has worked with special education middle schoolers, cofounded a play-based preschool, and worked in the nonprofit sector to provide healthy recreation options for children of all ages.

An outdoor enthusiast, Karen lives in Manchester Center, Vermont, with her husband and high school sweetheart, Michael, their two sons, and their dog and cat.

www.BalanceEducationalServices.com

Introduction

I found one day in school a boy of medium size ill-treating a smaller boy. I expostulated, but he replied: "The bigs hit me, so I hit the babies; that's fair." In these words he epitomized the history of the human race.
—BERTRAND RUSSELL

School used to be great. I loved it. Now I hate it. The kids are mean, everyone picks on me, and no one does anything about them.
—DANNY H., 5TH GRADE, 2005

Accepting bullying as an inevitable part of childhood is no longer tolerated. The customary responses, "Boys will be boys," and, "That's the way girls are," are outdated and ignore research that has shown the long-term negative impact bullying has on not only the bullied child, but also on the bully and those who witness bullying. Ongoing bullying leads to low self-esteem, criminal activity, domestic violence, suicide, and other self-destructive behaviors as well as distrust in the ability of authority to create and maintain a safe educational environment (Nansel, et al., 2001). It is for these reasons that most states in America have passed laws that require schools to address bullying.

While scientific evidence clearly backs up the need to address bullying, we do not need research to tell us that children are hurt by bullying. As educators, we have seen how bullying hurts children, robs them of relationships, and damages self-esteem.

We believe the issue of bullying should be addressed in a proactive fashion. To that end, we have designed fun and interactive activities that proactively teach behaviors that are expected in and out of school, including how to stand up to a bully, how to stop another student from bullying, and how to stop being a bully.

In most bullying situations, there are three groups represented: the bully, the targeted student, and the bystanders. While bullies set the bullying dynamic in motion, it is often the actions of the targeted student and the bystanders that determine whether the bullying is going to continue.

From the bully's perspective, bullying serves a function. Bullying either gets them something, helps them to avoid something, or is the only way the bully knows to get a need met. Students who bully others to get their needs met must learn new behaviors—replacement behaviors—which get their needs met without hurting others. If children who bully do not learn replacement behaviors, they will continue their abusive style as they grow into adulthood (Sarazen, 2002). When bullying students begin to date, bullying behavior often morphs into dating violence (Kendall-Tackett & Giacomoni, 2005). Further on, as the child becomes an adult, bullying behaviors and relationship violence are defined as domestic abuse. This behavior can also show up on the job as workplace harassment (Lutgen-Sandvick, Tracy, & Alberts, 2007).

Targets of bullying can go through a similar evolution. If a person who is chronically victimized doesn't learn to change how they respond to bullying behavior, they will continue to be targeted by bullies well into adulthood. For targets, replacement behaviors include learning how to limit their vulnerability to bullies by standing up to bullies in a nonviolent, yet assertive manner and by increasing their friendship network.

In spite of Bertrand Russell's quote, most students are not regular bullies or chronically targeted. Most students are bystanders—people who see, hear, or know about bullying. In one study, 95 percent of students reported witnessing verbal bullying, 68 percent witnessed physical bullying, and 48 percent of the secondary school students reported having witnessed physical sexual coercion (Rigby & Johnson, n.d.). Research has also shown that although bystanders sometimes speak out to discourage bullying, the most common response is to ignore what is going on—and the bullying simply continues (Bender, 2007). Students have to know how their school expects them to respond when they see bullying. It is the responsibility of school staff to teach all of our students how to fulfill those expectations in a manner that is responsible, yet acceptable to student culture.

Behaviors that perpetuate bullying need to be replaced with behaviors that are respectful, cooperative, compassionate, and empowering. The lessons and activities in this book will help accomplish this goal in a fun, interactive manner that also meets state curriculum guidelines.

HOW TO USE THIS BOOK

Throughout the lessons in this book you will note the use of common words and examples. However, in your community these same concepts may be expressed differently. Suggested script ideas, written in italics, are provided as examples of how the concepts we want to teach can be shared. If the words we chose are different from those used in your school, change the language but keep the concepts. Use words that complement your style of teaching and are relatable to your students. Make each lesson your own and unique to the students with whom you work. This book has been designed with large margins for your own notes and ideas about what works with your students.

Throughout the school year, it is important to have ongoing reminders of the values of empathy, friendship, and respect. Making time to practice role-playing throughout the year is much more effective than teaching a lesson once and moving on, never to revisit the concept again. Age-appropriate and individualized reinforcements on a randomized schedule will also increase pro-social behaviors.

In addition, role modeling is one of the most powerful teaching tools adults have. School staff are role models, and students will not only key in on what we say, but how we act. Educators and school staff must role model the same behaviors that are taught to students. When students do misbehave, it is an opportunity to role model and assertively enforce rules of behavior. Controlling emotions and acting respectfully when enforcing rules or imparting consequences is the most important type of role modeling and a very effective teaching style.

To reduce bullying, multiple strategies must be employed. The collective efforts of staff, students, and parents are needed to protect all children and to teach students the pro-social behaviors they will need throughout their lives. Current research finds the most effective schools curtail bullying by having:

- a comprehensive policy that details the definition of bullying and related behaviors that will incur consequences,
- a consistent staff response to all students who display such behavior,
- role modeling by educators of the behaviors they expect from students,
- discipline procedures designed to decrease bullying and increase desired behaviors, and
- reporting mechanisms that allow for all constituents to report bullying and maintain personal safety (Nelson, n.d.).

With policy and procedures that reflect the values of the school community, academic time will increase and behavioral skills will improve.

Keep in mind, the concepts taught in this book are not obvious to all or simply common sense. Pro-social skills need to be practiced by all students on a regular basis with extra practice time for those students who need additional help in perfecting these skills. The effectiveness of these lessons is contingent on keeping the lessons relatable to your students and the culture in which they live. Making the lessons fun, entertaining, and interactive will create an educational experience where all students—the bully, the bullied, and the bystander—pay attention and learn to use new behaviors both inside and outside the classroom setting.

. . . I talk to my elementary school students about the ways they handle stress and conflict. These students often say to me, "My daddy (or my mama) tells me that when someone hits me, I should hit back." When I ask my students to imagine other ways of responding to anger and bullying, they are silent.

If . . . children learn only to "hit back," we will see no end to extra police officers on the street, no end to rising murder rates. I ask today's citizen marchers, after you leave City Hall, please march to a school or a youth group and volunteer your strength, your wisdom, and your energy to our children. Show them a world beyond "hitting back."

—WHITNEY STEWART, CHILDREN'S BOOK AUTHOR,
THE TIMES-PICAYUNE, NEW ORLEANS, LOUISIANA,
LETTER TO THE EDITOR

"Same Page" Understanding of Violence, Respect, and Bullying

1

> *Tenderness and kindness are not signs of weakness and despair, but manifestations of strength and resolution.*
>
> —KAHLIL GIBRAN

Students, staff, and parents agree that violence should not be part of the school experience. However, the concept of bullying—how it is defined, behaviors that are considered bullying, and to what degree it is an acceptable part of childhood—varies from person to person. This ambiguity is one reason that many students bully without realizing that their actions are a type of bullying.

Having all staff, students, and parents agree on a common definition of violence, bullying, and other unacceptable behaviors can be challenging. Each person's unique life experience influences how they define violence and if and when violence is ever acceptable. These influences may include, but are not limited to:

- gender;
- age;
- urban, suburban, or rural upbringing;
- experience with bullying; and
- experience with domestic violence.

We don't have to like everyone, but we do need to treat everyone respectfully.

To lessen violent and bullying behaviors, students need to understand the definitions of violence and bullying as well as their various manifestations. Violent and bullying behaviors then need to be replaced with respect and other pro-social behaviors—behaviors that fulfill the bully's needs previously met through violence and bullying.

Instilling respect and citizenship is an aspect of every state curriculum. Most school administrators and classroom teachers talk about respect, expect respect, and put up posters encouraging respectful behavior. Students often hear, "Treat others with respect," "Use a respectful tone," "Respect your elders," and, "Talk to me with respect." It becomes obvious that respect is of value to adults. In fact, as a central concept in many ethical theories, respectful behavior is considered the very essence of morality and the foundation of all other moral duties and obligations.

However, many children, especially children who do not have respectful role models, do not know what adults, or the larger community, mean by respect. For these children, specific examples of respectful behaviors are not necessarily obvious or "no-brainers."

To encourage respectful, nonviolent behavior, students need to understand what respect looks and sounds like. Then, when students display respectful behaviors, staff need to make sure students are reinforced by acknowledging exactly what was appreciated and offer rewards that show their appreciation.

The following lessons will help develop a "same page" understanding of the types of behaviors the teacher and school community consider respectful, violent, and bullying.

DEFINING VIOLENCE

This lesson will define violence and demonstrate specific examples of behaviors considered violent. Some examples are obvious and others will generate debate.

Materials:
a one-liter water
   bottle filled
   with water
adult volunteer

GOAL: Students will understand what violence means and which behaviors are considered violent and unacceptable at school.

Time: 30 minutes

ACTIVITY

1 Ask a volunteer to get a dictionary or use the Internet to find the definition of violence. Ask the volunteer to give the definition only when requested. While this is happening, ask the other students what they think are the definitions of violence. Remember, you are not asking for examples, you want to define violence.

Ask the volunteer to read the definition; write the dictionary definition on the board. Common definitions include:

- physical force exerted for the purpose of violating, damaging, or abusing;
- abusive or unjust exercise of power;
- great roughness and force, often causing severe injury or damage; or
- in law: the unlawful use of physical force; intimidation by exciting fear that such force will be used.

2 Ask for a student volunteer to join you at the front of the class. State that you are going to pretend to hit the student but won't actually do it. Be sure that all students understand this is a demonstration and that you will not actually hit anyone. Making sure not to make physical contact, pretend to hit the student volunteer on the arm or head. Ask the class, *"If I hit someone, is it violence?"* Solicit opinions from the class. Ultimately, the answer is, "Yes, it is violence because it fits the definition of violence."

Continue the demonstration by saying and acting out, but not actually doing, the following; *"So, would it be considered violence if I pinch someone, pull their hair, flick their ear, kick them, push them, or poke them?"*

The concept that these behaviors would be considered violent is usually obvious. However, this discussion should make it clear to all students that touching or hitting another in a way that is undesired or hurtful will not be tolerated.

Have the student volunteer sit back down.

Students often bring up, "But what if . . . ?" and, "But what about . . . ?" questions. Discussing these questions ensures a greater chance of understanding and buy-in from your students. It also shows that the students are involved and thinking about the topic, but don't let the questions take over the whole lesson.

But What If . . . ?

"But what if you are playing two-hand touch football and you have to hit the person carrying the ball?"

After some discussion most students conclude there is a difference between hitting someone who doesn't want to be hit or is not expecting it and someone who expects to be touched. When you are playing football, or other sports, or just messing around with your friends, then contact is expected. This would be an acceptable behavior as long as it is not purposely hurtful and follows the rules. Remember, in sports there is a penalty for inappropriate touch or purposely hurtful contact.

3 Call up another student volunteer. Let the student and class know you will be acting out another scenario. Remind everyone that you will not actually hurt the volunteer or even touch the volunteer. Proceed to make believe you are throwing the one-liter water bottle (or something similar) at the volunteer. Instead of actually throwing the bottle, hold the bottle up in the air with one hand and walk quickly toward the student so that it looks like the bottle in your hand will hit the student—remember not to actually make contact.

Ask the class, *"If I purposely throw something at someone and hit them, is it violence?"* Solicit answers. After a brief discussion, inform the class the answer is yes, because someone might get hurt or feel intimidated.

But What If . . . ?

"But what if someone asks you to throw them an eraser or a ball? Is that violence?"

Answer the question with a demonstration of what appropriate throwing of an object to another looks and sounds like. Turn to the volunteer, call the student's name, and make eye contact. Indicate that you will be tossing the item, watch, and wait until the student puts their hands in a catching position. Then toss with the appropriate amount of force so that the item may be easily caught.

Ask the students if that action would be considered violence. Most will agree that it was not violence. Finally, make it clear that you called

Reminding all the students that you are just acting and will not really hurt anyone role models the importance of asking for trust and honoring that trust. Due to media influence, some students believe that doing the unexpected is actually funny and an indication of a good sense of humor. The unexpected often is funny, but not when someone's trust is violated.

the person's name, waited for a response, and then made sure the person was ready to catch what was being thrown. Only then did you toss the object, and in a manner that was easy for them to catch.

Remind the students that throwing something to someone who is not expecting it, doesn't want the object to be thrown at them, or throwing it much harder than expected is inappropriate, mean, and would be considered violent, disrespectful misbehavior.

Have the student volunteer sit back down.

If a student demonstrates a *pattern* of throwing or tossing objects in a disrespectful or violent manner, try a consequence that prohibits the student from throwing or tossing *anything* to another student until a staff member teaches and practices proper throwing or tossing techniques with different objects at various distances. This choice of consequence will help to determine if the student is actually lacking a skill or is purposely misbehaving. Either way, the student will learn the skill through role modeling and role-playing, and create a bond with an adult while having a positive learning experience. These benefits are very effective in replacing misbehavior with appropriate social skills.

4 Call up a third student volunteer. Remind the students this is a role-play and no one will be hurt. Stand about ten feet from the volunteer. Pretend that you are going to throw the water bottle, then carry it through the air toward the student, but past the student as if the bottle were whizzing right by the student's head.

Explain to the students that since you were only ten feet away, you could hit the volunteer if you wanted to, but you are purposely missing. Ask the class, "*Is it violence if I throw something near someone to scare them, but purposely miss?*" Discuss the student responses. This time expect to hear a combination of, "yes," "no," and, "it depends." Ask each respondent to explain why they answered the way they did. This discussion is a processing opportunity for the students and should be given ample time.

Ultimately remind the students that according to the definition used at the beginning of this lesson, it would be considered violence if it was meant to scare, threaten, or intimidate. Make it clear that such a threat or act of intimidation is unacceptable behavior on the school campus.

Students who have experienced domestic violence may view such threatening or intimidating behavior as common. It is possible they have been taught that physical contact is the difference between violence and nonviolence. These children may not easily accept that the *threat* of violence or intimidation would be considered violent. Private meetings with these children may be necessary to make sure they understand that threats will not be tolerated in the school or at any school-related function.

5 For the next scenario, ask an adult volunteer to act as the target. (Discuss this scenario with the adult before it is acted out.) If an adult is not available, use an inanimate object, such as a stuffed animal, a doll, or a drawing of a person. *Do not use a student volunteer.*

Act out the following:

Walk up to the adult volunteer, and with a harsh voice, a stern look, and a pointed finger, say, *"Hey you little nerd, you really bug me and I'm going to get you after school!"* Then powerfully turn and walk away.

Pause for a moment and then turn to the students and ask, *"Was that violence?"* After a brief discussion, make it clear the answer is yes, because of the threat of violence. This clear demonstration leads us to discuss a more ambiguous situation, which follows.

6 Stand as far from the adult volunteer as possible. Then, in a relatively soft tone—do not raise your voice, do not threaten—but one in which all can hear, say, *"Hey, would you please do me a favor? I really like you and think you're a pretty nice person. I was thinking about you. Would you please explain to all of us how you get dressed in the morning?"* Now, in a more condescending tone, add, *"I mean, let's face it; everyone knows you are not the brightest bulb in the box, always needing extra help and all. I'm sure we are all wondering how you get dressed in the morning. Do you have your mommy do it? Or do you have to hire someone to help you with your socks and undies?"*

The adult volunteer should just stand there looking sad and hurt. Pause to let the power of the moment settle.

Then ask the class if that was an example of violence. After a brief discussion, you will notice most students will respond, *"Yes, it is violence."* Challenge this response with, *"But I didn't yell or swear or threaten. In fact, I used polite words."* This is an opportunity for the students to formulate and articulate why they think such behavior is unacceptable.

But What About . . . ?

This time *you* ask the class, "*But what about 'Sticks and stones may break my bones, but names will never harm me?'*" This should generate a good discussion.

Activity: Other "Sticks and Stones" Sayings

Share the following sayings with the students:

"Sticks and stones may break my bones, but words can really, really hurt."

"Sticks and stones may break my bones . . . so don't throw sticks and stones."

Ask the students if they can think of other sayings.

But What If . . . ?

"But what if you are just kidding around with someone? You know, just teasing?"

Your response might include: "*Teasing is fun for* all *the people involved. It is not meant to embarrass someone or to be mean and hurtful. Teasing creates friendships and brings people closer together. The types of words used in the role-play were intended to humiliate, meaning it wasn't teasing or just kidding around. It was taunting or bullying.*" (See Chapter 8 on Playful Teasing vs. Hurtful Taunting.)

By the end of the discussion, make it clear that the comments you made to the adult volunteer had characteristics of violence by reviewing the definition of violence and pointing out that the statements were intended to abuse the person. Although being called names is different than being hit by a fist or a rock, name calling, put downs, and threatening violence are very hurtful and unacceptable on the school campus.

Final Thoughts

Tell the students you are not only talking about types of violence to make sure they don't act violently toward others, but to help them understand that they shouldn't accept it if they experience or witness violence. The lessons in Chapter 6, Responding to a Bully, and Chapter 7, The Power of Bystanders, will teach your students what do if they are a target or witness violent behaviors.

WHAT IS BULLYING AND RESPECT?

This lesson will have each student consider specific examples of respectful behavior as well as bullying and disrespectful behavior. The lesson is designed to exercise the students' critical thinking skills as well as offer adults the opportunity to articulate specific behaviors they want to encourage or diminish. In addition, students will gain a deeper insight into what their peers are thinking in regard to appropriate behavior. This insight may influence their actions through positive peer pressure.

Materials:
paper
pencil
dictionary

GOAL: Students will define and give specific examples of respect, disrespect, and bullying.

Time: 45 minutes

ACTIVITY

1 Ask a volunteer to get a dictionary or use the Internet to find the definition of bullying. Ask the volunteer to give the definition only when requested. While this is happening, ask the other students what they think are the definitions of bully and bullying. Remember, you are not asking for examples, you want to define bullying.

Ask the student who researched the word to read the definitions they found. Our dictionary has defined bully and bullying as follows:

Bully:
- a person who hurts or frightens other, weaker people
- a cruel and brutal person
- one habitually cruel to others who are weaker

Bullying:
- behavior that ridicules, humiliates, or harms another person; may be repeated over time
- to discourage or frighten with threats

- systematically and chronically inflicting physical hurt and/or psychological distress on one or more people
- to intimidate with superior strength

 Punctuate the conversation by stating that bullying is when a person or group of people use a power they have—such as physical, verbal, or social—to intimidate or hurt one or more people who have less power.

Suggested Script:

Bullying is when a person, or group of people, uses power—such as physical, verbal, or social—to harass or intimidate one or more people who have less power.

There are many different types of bullying, such as:

Physical: *Physical bullying is action oriented. It includes hitting, kicking, spitting, pushing, or taking or damaging a person's property.*

Verbal: *Verbal bullying is the use of words to hurt or humiliate another person. It includes name-calling, insulting, put-downs, and making threats or rude comments.*

Relational (also known as social aggression): *Relational bullying is the use of relationships to hurt others. It includes using the silent treatment, preventing people from playing with others, and spreading rumors and lies.*

Cyber: *Cyber bullying is the use of technology to hurt or humiliate others. It includes using computers and the Internet, e-mails, Instant Messaging (IM), cell phones (i.e., text messaging), and digital photography to embarrass or exclude others.*

2 Ask a different volunteer to look up the definition of respect. Ask the volunteer not to give out the definition until you call on them. While this is happening, ask the other students what they think are definitions of respect. Get approximately four definitions from the class and put them on the board.

Ask the student who researched the word what definitions they found. In our dictionary, respect is defined as:

Respect:
- a feeling of appreciation
- regarded with honor or esteem
- to show consideration or appreciation
- polite expressions

Historically, the word "bully" had positive meanings. However, today it means to abuse or harass another.

To find out if your state has a bullying law and a legal definition of the term bullying, check out http://www.bully police.org.

3 Discuss specific examples of what respect is, what it looks like, how it plays out, etc. Give a couple of examples, such as holding the door open for the next person, saying, "thank you," or, "excuse me," or picking up something that another person dropped. Many of these examples would be considered common courtesy. Come up with other interesting and not necessarily common examples as well, such as flushing the toilet after use, washing your hands after using the toilet, or quietly and politely telling someone that their pants are unzipped.

4 Next, hand out paper. On the board, create a chart such as the one shown in Figure 1.1 below. The students should do the same on their paper.

Figure 1.1

1 Respect	2 Disrespect	3 Bullying

Ask the students to write down two or three new examples of respect, disrespect, and bullying in the appropriate columns.

5 After the students complete their examples, go around the room and count off 1, 2, 3, 1, 2, 3, etc., so every student is a number 1, 2, or 3.

Taking turns is an example of respectful, cooperative behavior.

6 Start at one end of the room. The first group of numbers 1, 2, and 3 will all come to the board together. All "number ones" will write their example of respect, all "number twos" will write their example of disrespect, and all "number threes" will write their example of bullying. When a student sits down, for instance, a number one, the next number one will come up.

! If a student comes to the board and a previous person has already written their example on the board, ask the student to think of another example. If they can't come up with anything, ask them to make a check next to the example they were going to write to indicate that they thought of the same example.

Figure 1.2 below shows an example of student work:

Figure 1.2

1 Respect	2 Disrespect	3 Bullying
✓✓Saying "please" and "thank you"	Spreading rumors	Telling others not to be friends with the new kid
Asking someone if they need help or how they need help	Burping in someone's face	Every day you destroy someone's property
Burping quietly	✓Swearing at someone	✓✓Picking on someone
Being nice	Leaving your mess for someone else to clean up	Making someone cry

7 When everyone has had a turn, review what was written on the board. Some examples will be self-explanatory and some will need more discussion. Be as specific as possible. In other words, if a student writes in the respect column, "Be nice to your brother," ask what "nice" means, what "nice" looks like, or specific examples of "nice" behavior.

Final Thoughts

Beyond defining bullying, we need to have the long-term goal of encouraging respect. An effective way to accomplish this is for the staff to role model respectful behavior, especially during times of high stress.

Remember, catch your students being respectful. Try using the four-to-one rule, which suggests that teachers have at least four positive interactions with students or give students at least four positive comments for every negative or corrective comment. Research shows when teachers have at least four positive interactions with students for each negative or corrective interaction, appropriate behavior increases, inappropriate behavior decreases, and relationships between students and teacher improve.

GROUND RULES

Ground rules are agreements about expected behavior. This lesson is designed to take your students' understanding of various types of violence and incorporate it into their daily interactions. Since it is not practical to consider every example of how violence may be expressed, we offer four basic ground rules—meaning the *four basic things you may not hurt*.

 Materials per student: one half-sheet of letter-size paper pencil

 Time: 15–20 minutes

> **GOAL: Students will learn the four ground rules.**

ACTIVITY

1 Hand out a half-sheet of standard letter-size paper (approximately 8½" × 5½").

Say to the class, *"A ground rule is an agreement of expected behavior that everyone is expected to follow. In order to help us to get along with each other, we have four basic ground rules. Please write the following on your paper."*

Write on the board:

Ground Rules
I will not hurt:

1. Myself

Explain that it is unacceptable to hurt yourself, just like we may not hurt others. Ask the students if they can think of examples of hurting themselves. Examples may include:
- Saying hurtful things to yourself such as, "I am such an idiot," "I am such a loser," "I wish I was dead."
- Hurting yourself by hitting objects, such as punching or kicking walls or refrigerators, which can damage your hand or foot. (The part about damaging property comes later.)
- Pulling your hair out, scratching yourself deeply, or cutting yourself with a sharp object.

Sometimes, after discussing the dangers of hurting one-self with elementary students, important discoveries concerning young students who are engaging in such actions are brought to the attention of adults. Fortunately, this gives adults the opportunity to inter-cede and assist students in getting professional help.

2 Add ground rule number two to the list.

Ground Rules
I will not hurt:

1. Myself

2. Others

Explain that purposeful hurting or the threat of hurting another person is against the rules. The details of this type of hurting are explained in the earlier activity "Defining Violence." If you have not had that discussion with your students, read through the activity and incorporate the concepts covered into the conversation.

But What If . . . ?

But what if you have to hit someone to defend yourself?

Your response might include: *"Self-defense means you have no choice but to protect your body. And, you should use only enough force to protect your-self until you can safely remove yourself from the situation. As an example, if someone grabs you, you can push them off, or hit them if necessary, to get away. However, you don't have the right to beat them up. If you do, then you will also be blamed for being violent."*

3 Add ground rule number three to the list.

Ground Rules
I will not hurt:

1. Myself

2. Others

3. Animals

Purposeful hurting of animals is unacceptable. It is important to dis-cuss the difference between such behavior and acceptable activities such as hunting and fishing. Hunting and fishing are acceptable exceptions to the ground rules as long as certain rules are followed. In most states, there are rules in regard to hunter safety classes, getting a license, and hunting or fishing in season. Hunters and fishers are considered ethical and respectful if they kill in the least painful way possible and plan to use the meat or skin. Examples of unacceptable hurting of animals include:

- not caring about an animal's physical or emotional needs,
- enjoying causing animals pain, and
- using an animal as a negative outlet for one's own emotions.

Most students agree that hurting animals is wrong, but when offered specific examples of how some people have purposely hurt an animal, some students have admitted that they are guilty of such behavior. These hurtful behaviors include:

- being mean to a pet because of something that happened at school,
- killing insects or frogs just for fun or because others were doing it, and
- cutting up caterpillars or earthworms just to see them squirm.

Let the students know that if they have done this before, they should forgive themselves. However, they now know that such behavior is wrong and may even be against the law (all states have some form of animal cruelty law).

 Some children may come from families who have a different standard of how to treat animals. If this is an issue for a student, a private discussion may be warranted.

 Add ground rule number four to the list.

Ground Rules
I will not hurt:

1. Myself

2. Others

3. Animals

4. Property

Property is defined as something of value to someone. Examples may include a computer, a book, a shirt, a toy, a rock in someone's collection, etc.

Explain that sometimes you have to stop and think if something is someone's property or not. For instance, a log used as a border in someone's garden is that person's property, but a log rotting in the woods is not necessarily property. Another example might be a newspaper. If the newspaper is sitting on someone's desk, it should be considered someone's property. If it is in the school's recycle bin, it is no longer anyone's property.

Optional: At this point, the students should have written all four ground rules on their piece of paper. Ask them to take their paper and fold it in half. Then half again. And then a third time. Ask your students to take off their left shoe and place the piece of paper in the shoe. Have them put their shoe back on. Then say, *"After school, when your parents ask you what you learned in school today, take off your shoe, pull out your piece of paper and discuss the ground rules with them."*

Activity: Property or Not Property

Have students read the poem "Hector the Collector" by Shel Silverstein. Then have the students come up with their own lists of things that some might consider valuable and others might consider junk.

Final Thoughts

This chapter has explored behaviors that will not be tolerated at school. Remember, it is very important to teach and reinforce the specific behaviors you want to encourage.

Teaching lessons about violence and respect will increase your students' understanding of which behaviors are not acceptable and which behaviors are encouraged. These clearly defined concepts will decrease misbehavior and therefore increase teaching time. In addition, your students will understand that by following the ground rules, they will be happier and life will be more pleasant.

STATISTICS AND STUDIES

- Research has found that bullying is most likely to occur in schools where there is a lack of adult supervision during breaks, where teachers and students are indifferent to or accept bullying behavior, and where rules against bullying are not consistently enforced. (Olweus, Limber, & Mihalic, 1999)
- "Bullying is a complex phenomenon. It's not something that will go away with an easy, one-shot solution. And I think we're mistaken if we believe that one school assembly is going to do the trick, and if the school does that, they can say, 'Well we dealt with bullying this year. Great, let's move on.' In order to reduce

bullying at a school requires a culture change at the school [sic], requires all the adults and the students together saying, 'This is something that we don't accept, and we are going to look out for each other and report and talk about this as a form of peer abuse.' And one doesn't get that climate or culture change overnight. So I think the most effective programs are those that are very comprehensive, that involve not just the students and a classroom teacher but every adult at a school. The bus drivers should feel they have a role in bullying prevention, a cafeteria worker, certainly the parents should feel they have a role in helping to create a bully-free atmosphere at the school. So I think the best programs out there, and the data I think would support this, are very comprehensive." (Chamberlain, 2003)

- Seventy-four percent of eight- to eleven-year-old students said teasing and bullying occur at their schools. (Talking With Kids About Tough Issues: A National Survey of Parents and Kids, Kaiser Family Foundation and Nickelodeon, 2001)
- Forty-three percent of high school and 37 percent of middle school boys believe it is okay to hit or threaten a person who makes them angry. Nineteen percent of the girls agree. (2000 Report Card: Report #1, The Ethics of American Youth: Violence and Substance Abuse: Data & Commentary, Josephson Institute of Ethics, 2001)
- Eighty-seven percent of teens said school shootings are motivated by a desire to "get back at those who have hurt them." (Myers, 2001)
- Over the course of a year, nearly one-fourth of students across grades reported that they had been harassed or bullied on school property because of their race, ethnicity, gender, religion, sexual orientation or disability. (Austin, et al., 2002)
- Ten percent of students who drop out of school do so because of repeated bullying. (Weinhold & Weinhold, 1998)
- Dan Olweus, considered the father of bullying research and a professor of psychology at the University of Bergen (Norway), defines bullying as "exposing a person repeatedly, and over time, to negative actions on the part of one or more students." (Olweus, 1999)
- The Mayo Clinic and the *Journal of the American Medical Association* define bullying as a specific type of aggression in which:
  - the behavior is intended to harm or disturb,
  - there is an imbalance of power, with a more powerful person or group attacking a less powerful one, and
  - the behavior occurs repeatedly over time. (Mayo Clinic, 2001)
- "In the past, bullying behavior was dichotomized—students were classified as either bullies or victims, but, kids [often] report that they're both." (Crawford, 2002)

Solving Problems Peacefully and Resolving Conflicts Respectfully

2

> *Ah, people asking questions, lost in confusion—well I tell them there's no problem, only solutions.*
>
> —John Lennon

By its nature, friendship involves conflict. Students need to know that relationships of all kinds include conflict. Some people avoid conflict fearing that confronting the issue or a person will cause anguish, discomfort, or the end of a relationship. Many students do not realize that avoiding conflict may result in pent-up emotions, unhealthy choices, direct bullying, or social aggression.

> **❗** Not everyone realizes that relationships naturally include conflict. Students need to know this so they can be prepared emotionally and intellectually to accept and resolve conflicts respectfully.

Students need to understand that confrontation does not cause conflict; it resolves conflict. When used effectively, confrontation can make a friendship stronger by showing the people involved they care enough about the relationship to work through differences. Knowing and accepting that conflict is a normal part of friendship helps a person prepare for this challenge. Students need to understand that when conflicts arise, it doesn't mean there is anything wrong with either person, nor does it have to lead to disrespectful or violent behavior. There is an alternative to going from best friends to worst enemies, but finding that place does not always come naturally. Understanding how to address conflict teaches students that friendships and other relationships can endure conflict without aggressive behaviors.

This chapter offers techniques to teach students how to solve their personal problems, resolve their conflicts, and address daily challenges effectively, respectfully, and peacefully. It is a proactive lesson intended to help students determine the best course of action when problems or conflicts arise or they are confronted with a situation that might develop into name-calling, physical fighting, or social aggression.

Teaching problem solving and conflict resolution strategies reduces arguments, power struggles, and social aggression by reinforcing the concepts of mutual respect, assertive communication, self-esteem, self-reliance, resilience, and emotional management.

> *Conflict is an inevitable part of childhood, and not all conflict is harmful or bad. Destructive conflict damages relationships, creates bad feelings, and leads to future problems. But constructive conflict helps children to learn, grow, and change for the better. They become more open-minded and tolerant, and they learn to see things from other perspectives.*
> — Allison Seale, Hamilton Fish Institute

THE FIVE STEPS OF SOLVING PROBLEMS PEACEFULLY AND RESOLVING CONFLICTS RESPECTFULLY

This activity teaches a five-step process for solving problems and resolving conflicts. Understanding and practicing this process will increase the chance that students will use these skills when confronted with problems and conflicts. To teach the lesson, we use a realistic inbounds/out-of-bounds recess conflict scenario relevant to most elementary-age students. The scenario is a situation that may lead to name-calling, intimidation, and fighting *or,* when resolved effectively, a compromise that both sides can agree to in order to continue the game. The odds that a pleasant outcome will occur are greatly enhanced if the students have practiced skills in emotional control and conflict resolution.

One day, when I was about 10, I was playing with a friend at his house. We argued about how long one of us was playing with a toy we were supposed to share. His mother came into the room, put her hand up to her neck, and declared, "I'm fed up to here with the two of you. Work it out or I'll take that toy away and no one will play with it!" Then she went back to the other room. I understood that my friend's mom wanted us to stop arguing and work it out, but we had absolutely no idea how to "work it out." I do remember thinking that instead of yelling at us, it would have been more helpful if my friend's mom would have taught us how to "work it out."

—SB

Materials
per group:
8½ × 11 paper
pencil
conflict cards
   (see Resource A)

GOAL: Students will learn how to solve problems and resolve conflicts.

Time: 60 minutes

ACTIVITY

1 Suggested Script:

In all relationships, friendships included, there are bound to be conflicts. Conflicts are disagreements between people. And some of these conflicts, or disagreements, may cause very strong emotions. It is important to know that as much as we might care about our friends, there will be times of conflict. We are going to learn how to resolve conflicts so that we can better get along with classmates, family, friends, and teammates. It is a skill that can help us get along with others and make life more pleasant.

Solving problems and resolving conflicts focus on solutions and similarities instead of problems and differences. Experiencing problems or conflicts with other people, and especially a person we are close to, is not pleasant, but it happens; it's a part of life. But it doesn't mean there has to be fighting, disrespectful, or painful behavior. There are

Friends treat each other with respect even when they are angry with each other.

ways to solve problems and resolve conflicts peacefully and perhaps make the relationship even stronger than it was before the conflict.

Therefore, knowing how to resolve conflicts will make your life and friendships much more enjoyable. And, if the conflict does change the friendship, you don't have to go from best friends to worst enemies.

We are going to learn a five-step process to resolve conflicts peacefully, using a common issue.

② Describe the following scenario to your students. Suggested Script:

It is lunch time and a group of students is playing soccer on the recess field. Everyone is having fun and taking the game seriously. The game is tied; the ball is kicked down the field, far from the students, near the imaginary out-of-bounds line. The game stops as one team says the ball went out of bounds and they get to throw it in to one of their players to restart the game; the other team says it didn't go out of bounds and they should continue play.

③ On the board, write:
The Five Steps of Conflict Resolution:

1. **Define the Problem or Conflict**
2. **Brainstorm Ideas**
3. **Weigh the "Pros" and "Cons" of Each Idea**
4. **Decide Plan "A"**
5. **Decide Backup Plan "B"**

Explain the steps, one by one, as described below.

1. Define the Problem or Conflict

Suggested Script:

The first step to solving a problem, or resolving a conflict, is to clearly define what the problem or conflict is about. If you don't clearly identify the main problem or conflict, it is hard to know when you've solved it.

  For many, defining the conflict is not an obvious place to begin.

You can illustrate the importance of defining the conflict in an entertaining way by acting like a student who does not stay focused on the problem. For instance, act like a student who rants about another student with an opposing view of where the ball rolled. Say things that will cause more problems instead of restarting the game. For instance:

> *The ball was inbounds! You always say whatever is best for you or your team! You don't play fair. You never do. You did this last week, too. Everybody knows that you cheat. You cheat at all the games. No one wants to play with you. You're not going to have any friends. Nobody likes cheaters!*

After the students stop laughing—because you are funny and they can really relate to your demonstration—state that if you do begin to lose focus on the main problem or conflict, the first thing you have to do is calm down (discussed further in Chapter 4, Emotional Control and Anger Management). Only when calm can a person solve a problem or resolve a conflict peacefully, respectfully, and efficiently.

Ask the students what they believe to be the problem or conflict in the described scenario. After soliciting opinions, state that you think the problem is the two teams disagree on where the ball rolled.

Physical Reminder: A Strategy intended to Assist Memory

Use physical reminders as a strategy to help students remember the five steps of solving problems peacefully and resolving conflicts respectfully. When students are experiencing a problem or conflict, or come to you for assistance, physical reminders help students remember the five steps.

 Older students may think physical reminders are goofy. Explain that when something is goofy, like a goofy TV commercial, there is a better chance that you will remember it. This acknowledgment gets buy-in from students who are self-conscious about looking silly.

Physical Reminder for Step 1: Define the Problem or Conflict

Put hands out in front of the body, palms up, and with a shrug of the shoulders ask, *"What's the problem, dude?"* This silly variation of a common phrase is used to remind students to focus on the main issue to be resolved. Note: Sometimes the physical movement without the stated question is enough of a Step 1 reminder.

Figure 2.1

2. Brainstorm Ideas

Once the problem or conflict is determined, it is time to brainstorm ideas. We have found that students come up with many ideas when they are not presently experiencing intense emotion or focused strictly on self-image, such as when they are experiencing an actual conflict.

Suggested Script:

> *Brainstorming is a technique for solving problems and conflicts. During brainstorming, we come up with many ideas to solve the problem. Every idea is acceptable. Brainstorming is not the time to judge or act on ideas—it is the time to be creative and generate ideas.*

Ask the students to brainstorm ideas on how to resolve the soccer game conflict. For this scenario, ideas may include (but are not limited to):

- Call a "do over."
- Stop playing the game.
- The person who was closest to the ball determines if the ball went out of bounds.
- Do a "drop in" (one player drops the ball between two players and the game continues from that point).
- The team that is losing gets the ball (if the score is not tied).
- Whoever grabs the ball first gets it for their team.
- Biggest kids get to decide.
- Let a teacher decide.
- Fight it out.
- Ask someone else to help brainstorm some ideas.

Write each idea the students brainstorm on the board. The goal is to teach them to open their minds to all possibilities, even to ideas that seem to be, or might really be, unacceptable. Therefore, if you find that no one comes up with something like "fight it out," offer an example like that yourself. Explain that we all have these types of destructive ideas and it is OK to think them, but not to act on them. By doing so, it opens up the mind to even more *good* ideas. Again, remind the students brainstorming is not the time to judge ideas or act upon them.

Students also need to be taught to limit their violent ideas. If a student offers five different violent ideas, such as kill, hit, smash, destroy, and kick, ask the student to state only one idea that covers all the variations. That way, you have shown you value their brainstorming, but teach the importance of coming up with *various* ideas instead of one idea with many different descriptions.

Physical Reminder for Step 2: Brainstorm Ideas

Put fingers on head and flick them outwards (see Figure 2.2). Like flashes of lightening, new ideas are storming out of the brain.

Figure 2.2

3. Weigh the "Pros" and "Cons" of Each Idea

Suggested Script:

> *The purpose of this step is to consider the "pros" and "cons" of each brainstormed idea. Pros and cons refer to the positives and negatives, or the good aspects and the bad aspects of each idea.*
>
> *Each idea has some pro sides and some con sides. The goal is to determine which idea has the best chance to resolve the conflict with the least chance of making the situation worse or creating a new problem.*

As a class, review each idea for its advantages and disadvantages. For example:

- Call a "do over."
  Pro: You can continue to play from the last neutral place on the field.
  Con: One team may have lost an advantage they thought they had.

- Stop playing the game.
  Pro: No more disagreement.
  Con: No one is playing soccer anymore.

- The person who was closest to the ball determines if the ball went out of bounds.
  Pro: It might be the best chance of getting the call right; you can continue to play.

Con: The person who was closest might lie.

- Do a "drop in."
  Pro: Equal for both sides.
  Con: One team may have lost an advantage they thought they had.

- Team that is losing gets the ball.
  Pro: Gives the team that is losing an advantage; you can continue to play.
  Con: It's not fair for the winning team to lose an opportunity.

- Whoever grabs the ball first gets it for their team.
  Pro: You can continue to play.
  Con: People might fight trying to grab the ball.

- Biggest kids get to decide.
  Pro: You can continue to play.
  Con: Smaller players may feel it is an unfair way to decide.

- Let a teacher decide.
  Pro: Teacher will probably be fair and neutral.
  Con: Teacher may not be available to help or was not watching.

- Fight it out.
  Pro: It might feel good to hit someone or call them a hurtful name.
  Con: You might get hurt or get into trouble; players probably won't be allowed to play anymore; punishment at school and home for violent behavior.

- Ask someone else to brainstorm some ideas.
  Pro: Another person may offer solutions you didn't think of.
  Con: It may take too much time to find another person; you may not like their ideas.

Consider the developmental ability of your students to determine how much time you need to spend on each idea. During the learning phase, the pro and con process may take a while. Once the skill is mastered, it moves along at a much faster speed.

A vital aspect of solving problems is to make situations better and to avoid making matters worse or creating a new problem.

After going through the pros and cons of each idea, ask the students if there is any idea that would obviously make the situation worse, or is unrealistic or illegal. Put a slash through those ideas, instead of erasing them, as a reminder that the ideas were discussed, but removed from consideration as possible solutions. In this example, "fight it out" would get a slash because it would make the situation worse.

In addition, some ideas have cons that are not much of a negative at all, so the con is rather small. If there is not much negative to the con, it is a clue that the positive aspect outweighs the negative aspect and the idea should be considered a good option.

Physical Reminder for Step 3: Weigh the "Pros" and "Cons" of Each Idea

Extend a closed hand and show a "thumbs up" for pro and a "thumbs down" for con.

Figure 2.3 _____ Figure 2.4 _____

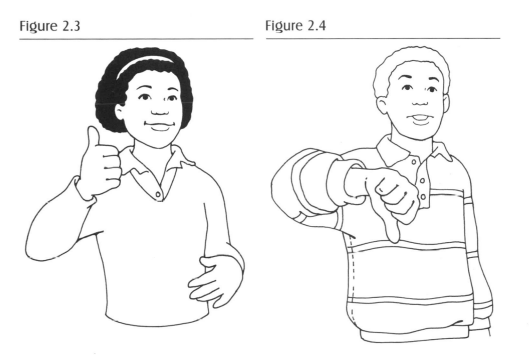

4. Decide Plan "A"

(Both Step 4 and Step 5 will be discussed before asking the students for their input.)

Suggested Script:

After discussing the pros and cons of each idea, it is time to decide which action to take to solve the problem or resolve the conflict. Plan "A" should be the idea that appears to have pros with the most advantages and cons with consequences that are neither severe nor would make the problem worse if the plan doesn't work out successfully.

 A good plan is one that has a strong chance of achieving the goal and few negative consequences if it doesn't achieve the goal. A bad plan is a plan that has a consequence that will create new and possibly worse problems.

Physical Reminder for Step 4: Decide Plan "A"

Show the American Sign Language letter "A."

5. Decide Backup Plan "B"

Suggested Script:

> *Of course, plans don't always work out the way you expect. Plan "A" may not succeed or others involved may not approve of your Plan "A." Therefore, it is wise to be prepared and have a backup plan ready. That would be Plan "B."*

Physical Reminder for Step 5: Decide Backup Plan "B"

Show the American Sign Language letter "B."

4 1. Ask a student which idea would be their choice for Plan "A" if they were in the situation involving the soccer game. Write an "A" next to that idea on the board. Then ask the same student, "If that doesn't work, what would be your Plan 'B'?" Write a "B" next to the idea.

2. Ask another student what their Plan "A" and Plan "B" would be. State that it may be exactly the same as the first student's Plan "A" or "B," or it might be different; each individual has to decide what plans they believe are best. Put an "A" and a "B" next to the choices of this second student, differentiating them from the first student with a different color chalk or marker, or by circling the letter. Go through the same process with three or four students.

! If neither Plan "A" nor "B" solves the problem or resolves the conflict, you might have to go to Plan "C" or "D." If you get to Plan "E" without success, it's time to get assistance.

---

5 **Small Group Activity**

This activity, as described, is designed for fourth grade and up. It can easily be adapted for younger students by having an adult lead the discussion and write down the ideas and the pros and cons.

The students should now be ready to practice solving a problem or resolving a conflict in small groups. This is an opportunity for students to consider and solve everyday issues that can lead to serious disruption in learning, emotional distress, bullying, and social aggression.

1. Explain that each group is to follow the five steps of problem solving to come up with a peaceful and respectful solution to their problem or conflict.

2. Review the five steps.

3. Divide the class into groups of three to four students. Each group will need one sheet of paper and a pencil. In each group assign a scribe to write down the ideas and pros and cons.

4. Hand out a conflict card to each group. Note: Conflict cards are available at the back of the book as Resource A on page 157.

5. Remind all the students that brainstorming includes all ideas, even the ideas another group member thinks is silly or might not work. Tell everyone you expect they will show respect by accepting an idea, writing it down, and then moving on to the next idea. Remind the students that brainstorming an idea does not mean you should do the idea. In addition, tell the students that there should be no more than two violent ideas per brainstorm session.

When dividing the students into groups, be aware of personal dynamics. Do not combine students who are presently experiencing a conflict. Also, consider students who are known as cool, responsible, and mature peer leaders, good at solving problems and resolving conflicts, i.e., high status students. Incorporate those students into various groups so their brainstorming and decision-making skills can be shared with other students who are not as experienced.

---

6. After each group has selected a Plan "A" and a Plan "B," you can choose either of the following:
   a. Privately discuss the solutions with each group, sharing your thoughts and opinions about their solutions. The benefit of discussing the solutions privately is that you can have the groups exchange conflict cards and each group can then practice with a new conflict.
   b. Have each group state their problem and share solutions with the class. This is a good sharing time, but other students

might get bored listening to a group's problems and solutions, so keep the sharing short and to the point.

 Practicing conflict resolution skills with various scenarios over numerous days is more effective than solving many problems in one day.

Problems and Conflicts to Resolve

The following problems are conflicts that could arise and lead to arguments, misunderstandings, fighting, bullying, and social aggression. Brainstorming other potential conflicts with your students can be very useful and insightful into issues specific to them.

1. Others won't let you join the soccer game (or basketball, football, etc.).

2. You want to use the swings, but they are all occupied.

3. A partner in your group project is not doing the work they are supposed to do.

4. Kids on top of the playground bars won't make room for you or let you up.

5. You put a lot of effort into drawing a picture and someone laughed at it.

6. Someone is saying bad things about one of your family members.

7. Someone keeps calling you an insulting name.

8. Friends won't share the ball or the jump rope with you.

9. A group of kids tells you that you cannot sit at their lunch table.

10. Someone messed up your nice shirt or pants.

11. Someone keeps making fun of the way you look.

12. A person in the car is smoking, and it is bothering you.

13. You want to go to the movies, but your friend wants to go to the mall.

14. You want to sleep over at a friend's house. Your parents say no.

15. Friends are doing things that you don't think are healthy (smoking, hanging out with a rough crowd, snorting sugar, using inhalants, etc.).

16. Someone keeps sending you nasty e-mails or IMs (instant messages).

17. A friend is saying hurtful things about another friend of yours.

18. You have been invited to two different parties on the same night.

19. You are invited to join a fun game with friends, but the friend you are with is not invited.

20. A classmate rolls their eyes when you speak during class.

> *Confrontation does not cause conflict—it resolves it. If you don't care enough about a relationship to resolve a problem, then there is no relationship. Eventually the problem will become so big that it can no longer be ignored. If you always avoid confrontation, the only resolution left is accepting that you are in an unhealthy relationship or leaving the relationship altogether. What kind of friend makes you feel that you weren't even worth a few moments of discomfort to say, "Hey, can we talk about this?" Or worse, we have the confrontation, but the friendship wasn't worth trying to move past the problem. That was the limit? I disagreed with you about something and now I have no value? That's not what I call a real friendship.*
>
> —JANET PHIPPS, SPECIAL EDUCATION TEACHER

Final Thoughts

Problem solving and conflict resolution are necessary skills in life—be it school, the community, or the workplace. For some, the concepts and skills of problem solving, conflict resolution, brainstorming, decision making, compromise, and sharing may seem easy and obvious. But these skills are not commonsense or obvious to everyone. These are skills that have to be role modeled, taught, practiced, and constructively critiqued.

The more often students practice solving real issues in a nonemotional setting, such as during class when conflict is not really occurring, the better the chance they will solve their problems and resolve their conflicts peacefully and respectfully in real situations. In actual situations, strong emotions may influence how a person addresses a challenging situation. Chapter 4, Emotional Control and Anger Management, offers lesson plans on how to teach students to recognize physical cues that indicate they are experiencing intense emotions and how to maintain self-control.

STATISTICS AND STUDIES

- Although the tendency may be to perceive the bully as merely an enemy in our anti-bullying strategy, he or she also suffers a tremendous potentially negative impact from the act of bullying. For instance, consider what the bully learns when his or her behavior is left unchecked and unchallenged by adults who may not understand the harm being done. The bully learns that such behavior is acceptable or even encouraged; that might does equal right. Moreover, if left unchecked, it may lead to their attempting greater crimes in the future. Bullies are four times more likely to be convicted criminals by the age of twenty-four. (Aldrich, 2001)

- Many children enter school with an understanding of what is expected of them in social situations involving emotional expression. These children have a strong sense of self-efficacy that allows them to try out new strategies in interpersonal situations (Saarni, 1999). These children are not concerned about evaluation of their behavior by others. They are confident in their ability to evaluate a situation and respond with an appropriate display of emotions and behaviors. From *What Everyone Should Know About Bullying and Violence*, at http://cyc-net.org/cyc-online/cycol-0603-empathy.html

- "I address bullying by sharing examples of situations that would be challenging and then use brainstorming, role play, and discussion to help students find alternative ways to solve the problem."
  —Cheryl Dellasega, author of *Girl Wars*
  (2003, Fireside Publishers) and
  Surviving Ophelia (2001, Perseus Publishing)

- "One testament of a good friendship is how friends deal with differences and conflicts. It's easy to believe you are good friends when you agree on an issue. It is when friends disagree that you can really determine the depth of the relationship. If you can have conflicts or arguments, yet still maintain mutual respect and remain friends, then you know you really have a special friend."
  —Unknown

Creating Empathy 3

> *I do not ask how the wounded person feels. I simply become that wounded person.*
>
> —WINSTON CHURCHILL

Empathy is a vital aspect of emotional intelligence. If our children are to communicate effectively and develop satisfying interpersonal relationships, it is essential that we help them develop empathy.

Empathy is the ability to feel what others are feeling. Empathy is the identification with, and the understanding of, another's situation, emotions, and motives. In other words, it is the ability to see the world through that person's eyes. Empathy influences us to treat others with respect and kindness; in turn it reduces violence and cruelty to others.

Most people are born with the ability to be empathetic. However, certain life experiences may diminish that ability. Children who have experienced domestic violence or some other form of abuse are especially at risk for diminished empathy.

Research supports the inclusion of empathy training to increase empathetic feelings and increase pro-social behavior. In addition, research shows an impressive correlation between students' training and skills in empathetic understanding and their academic performance.

An increase in empathy will develop over time through role modeling from many adults and consistent reminders.

WHAT MAKES YOU FEEL . . . ?

Emotions tend to arise spontaneously, rather than through conscious thought or effort and are often accompanied by physiological changes. Emotions are neither good nor bad; they are just a natural part of life. How one expresses emotions, however, will be judged by society as good or bad, acceptable or unacceptable.

The purpose of this lesson is for students to recognize and verbalize their emotions. To increase empathy for others we first focus on having the students gain greater self-awareness and learn to value their own emotions.

 Materials per student:
paper
pencil

GOAL: Students will recognize and accept their emotions.

 Time: 20–30 minutes

ACTIVITY

1 Write on the board the following definition of empathy:
Empathy is:
- the ability to feel what others are feeling
- to see the world through another person's eyes
- to identify and understand another's situation or emotions

Say, *"Empathy, or being empathetic, means you understand how another person feels about a situation. In order to understand how others feel, we need to be aware of our feelings."*

2 Next, hand out paper to the students. Ask the students to write their answers to the following questions. Let them know that you will not be collecting their papers and that their answers will remain private.

On the board write, "What makes you feel . . . ?" (See Figure 3.1).

1. **happy?** (An example of an answer would be, "When I go out to eat.")

After the students have written their answers, then write:

2. **mad?**

Again, after the students have written their answers, write:

3. **sad?**

Repeat this process for the next three:

4. **nervous?**

5. **excited?**

6. **frustrated?**

Figure 3.1

> What Makes You Feel....
> 1) HAPPY?
>
> 2) MAD?
>
> 3) SAD?

These words are examples of emotion words. You don't have to start out with this amount or these specific emotions. Consider how many emotion questions are appropriate for the time you have allotted and the developmental age of your students.

> **!** If the students are too young to write, or writing will take too long, this activity may be done sitting in a circle with the students answering the questions aloud. Always tell the students they may say, "Pass," if they choose not to answer the question. This shows respect for their feelings of shyness and/or privacy.

3 After the students have finished writing, ask for volunteers to share their answers with the class. As the students answer, delve deeper into their responses. For example, if a student says, "I get happy when I see my dog," or, "I feel mad when I am not allowed to go to my friend's house," follow up by asking the student to verbalize why they feel this way. This is an opportunity for students to gain a deeper understanding of their own feelings and the feelings of others while improving their verbal and listening skills.

Asking "why" is key to this activity. We are asking the students to have a deeper awareness of their own emotions.

Use emotion words as vocabulary and/or spelling words for the week. This strategy reinforces the value placed on emotional awareness.

Final Thoughts

The purpose of this lesson has been to increase the students' recognition and appropriate verbal expression of their emotions. You can support this lesson with ongoing conversations about their emotions by using emotion words to fulfill spelling and vocabulary requirements. In addition to asking students how to spell or define a particular emotion word, take a few moments to ask what makes them experience that emotion. This strategy reinforces the value placed on emotional awareness.

Lesson Extension

Some emotion words might include the following:

1. acquiescent
2. adequate
3. affectionate
4. afraid
5. aggressive
6. alarmed
7. alone
8. amazed
9. ambitious
10. amused
11. angry
12. anguish
13. animosity
14. annoyed
15. anxious
16. apathetic
17. appreciated
18. apprehensive
19. ardent
20. ashamed
21. assured
22. awestruck
23. awkward
24. bad
25. belonging
26. benevolent
27. bewildered
28. bitter
29. blissful
30. bored
31. brave
32. bullied
33. caring
34. cautious
35. cheerful
36. close
37. competent
38. competitive
39. concerned
40. confident
41. confused
42. contemptuous
43. contented
44. controlling
45. cool
46. cordial
47. cowardly
48. cranky
49. cross
50. curious
51. defeated
52. defensive
53. dejected
54. delighted
55. delirious
56. dependence
57. depressed
58. desired
59. devoted
60. disappointed
61. discontented
62. discouraged
63. disgusted
64. disheartened
65. dismayed
66. dispassionate

67. disrespectful
68. distant
69. distress
70. distrustful
71. docile
72. down
73. eager
74. earnest
75. ecstasy
76. edgy
77. elated
78. embarrassed
79. empty
80. enjoyment
81. enthusiastic
82. envious
83. excited
84. exhausted
85. expectant
86. fair
87. faithful
88. fascinated
89. fear
90. fearful
91. flowing
92. forceful
93. forgiving
94. fractious
95. frantic
96. free
97. friendly
98. frivolous
99. frustrated
100. furious
101. gentle
102. good
103. grateful
104. gratitude
105. greedy
106. grief
107. guilty
108. happy
109. hassled
110. hate
111. hatred
112. helpless
113. hope
114. hopeful
115. hopeless
116. hostile
117. humble
118. humiliation
119. humorous
120. hurt
121. hysterical
122. icky
123. impassive
124. impatient
125. impulsive
126. inadequate
127. independent
128. indifferent
129. inferior
130. insecure
131. inspired
132. interested
133. intolerant
134. involved
135. irritated
136. jealous
137. joy
138. joyful
139. kind
140. lazy
141. left out
142. lighthearted
143. lonely
144. lost
145. loved
146. loving
147. mad
148. masterful
149. meek
150. melancholic
151. miserable
152. mistrusting
153. needed
154. neglected
155. nervous
156. neutral
157. noninvolved
158. nostalgic
159. obedient

160. optimistic
161. passionate
162. passive
163. pathetic
164. patient
165. peaceful
166. pessimistic
167. philosophical
168. pitiful
169. pleasant
170. pleased
171. poetical
172. pompous
173. possessive
174. powerful
175. protective
176. proud
177. provocative
178. put down
179. rage
180. rapturous
181. rebellious
182. reckless
183. regretful
184. rejected
185. relaxed
186. relieved
187. reluctant
188. remorse
189. remorseful
190. repulsed
191. resentful
192. resilient
193. respectful
194. responsible
195. responsive
196. restful
197. restrained
198. revolted
199. ridiculous
200. righteous
201. romantic
202. sad
203. satisfied
204. secure
205. self-blaming
206. self-conscious
207. sensitive
208. serene
209. shame
210. shamed
211. shocked
212. shy
213. silly
214. sincere
215. small
216. smug
217. sorry for self
218. spiteful
219. startled
220. stimulated
221. stoical
222. stressed
223. stubborn
224. sulky
225. superior
226. surprised
227. suspicious
228. sympathetic
229. temper
230. tense
231. terrified
232. threatened
233. thrilled
234. tired
235. tolerant
236. tranquil
237. triumphant
238. troubled
239. trusting
240. uncaring
241. uncertain
242. uneasy
243. unfair
244. unkind
245. unneeded
246. unpleasant
247. unsettled
248. wary
249. zesty
250. zippy

FIND THE EMOTION WORDS

Figure 3.2

Find the Emotion Words

```
N  X  M  X  D  N  J  J  M  D  C  Q  D  D  T
O  G  L  I  U  E  A  O  I  E  A  A  E  O  E
I  S  K  V  S  N  L  S  Y  I  M  T  S  I  R
T  U  K  V  G  E  T  T  O  W  A  V  U  X  R
A  R  T  E  D  R  R  K  R  R  Z  D  F  D  O
I  P  R  E  E  A  T  A  T  A  S  F  N  K  R
L  R  E  S  I  S  N  S  B  D  T  O  O  G  N
I  I  S  J  U  T  U  G  X  L  U  S  C  Z  S
M  S  N  G  R  R  I  S  U  T  E  O  C  W  D
U  E  S  A  F  D  E  V  E  I  L  E  R  L  E
H  I  E  R  A  G  E  M  A  H  S  T  X  P  V
D  F  K  J  R  I  R  D  B  C  T  H  E  I  O
J  B  D  B  P  H  R  V  J  W  M  N  J  N  L
R  L  M  O  N  Z  E  X  C  I  T  E  D  A  B
E  N  J  O  Y  M  E  N  T  E  Z  G  W  I  S
```

ANGER	ANGUISH	CONFUSED
DISGUST	DISTRESS	ENJOYMENT
EXCITED	FEAR	FRUSTRATED
HUMILIATION	JOY	LOVED
MISERABLE	PROUD	RAGE
RELIEVED	SHAME	STARTLED
SURPRISE	TERROR	

Create Your Own Find-A-Word and Other Puzzles
Use the Internet to create your own word search, cryptograms, or crossword puzzles. Go to http://puzzlemaker. discoveryeducation. com

WORD SCRAMBLE

On the board, write the scrambled letters of one emotion word; for instance, dsa (sad), or hyapp (happy), or sdacre (scared). On a piece of paper, have the students (or a group of two or three students) unscramble the words. Ask the students to wait to be called upon before stating their answer.

It is a sign of respect to raise your hand and wait to be called upon before answering a question.

Variation

Write each letter of an emotion word on a separate index card, as in Figure 3.3. This will make one "set" of cards. Do this for several words so that each set of index cards contains the letters of only one word. Hand each set to a student or a group of two or three students. Have them spread out the letters of each set and determine what the word is supposed to be.

Figure 3.3 shows an example of a word scramble.

Figure 3.3

This is a fun game and the students will enjoy unscrambling the words. You might find they are better at this game than expected, especially with longer words (frustrated, confident, etc.).

Take time to discuss the definitions of the words and why a person may feel that emotion.

EMOTIONAL STATUES—
RECOGNIZING BODY LANGUAGE

The Emotional Statues activity helps students recognize how their emotional states affect their bodies. It also helps them to recognize the physical cues their bodies are giving them to indicate their overall emotional state or how they are feeling about a specific issue. For example, when Jamal gets nervous, he scrunches his face and his stomach gets queasy. At that point he begins to bite his nails. By learning the cues that precede his nail biting, he can avoid nail biting. This will be discussed further in "Feeling Clouds and Charades" on page 51.

Emotional Statues also increases empathy by teaching students to recognize others' body language and what emotions another person might be experiencing. By recognizing physical cues that another might be upset, nervous, angry, etc., a student will be better able to determine how to treat that person respectfully. For example, if Juan recognizes the cues that Patrice may be getting angry when he is teasing her, Juan will know that he should stop teasing and perhaps even apologize.

Materials:
none

 Time: 15 minutes

> **GOAL: Students will recognize the physical cues of their own emotional states and the emotional states of others.**

ACTIVITY

1 Suggested Script:

The purpose of this activity is to understand how people communicate their emotions using their faces and bodies. When people communicate their emotions using their faces and bodies, it is called body language. By understanding people's body language, we can understand what emotions they are feeling.

In a moment, you are going to walk around the room. You are to walk around respectfully, not bumping into people or objects, and you will need to be visible to others.

2 Indicate any areas that are off limits. *As you walk around the room, I am going to call out an emotion word. When you hear the word, turn toward the middle of the room and strike a pose that shows that emotion. Remember, statues are still and make no noise.*

For example, if I call out "happy," you would freeze and show what happiness looks like using your face and body. Then strike a pose that shows a big, but not overly exaggerated, expression of happiness. *In my example of happiness, I am smiling and you can see the whites of my eyes. I am showing my teeth, there are lines by my eyes, and my cheeks go up. My shoulders are back and my chest is out. As you strike this pose, I will name the details of the body language and facial expressions I see.*

3 After explaining the activity, have the students get up and walk around. To begin, call out the more obvious words such as happy, sad, mad, proud, and nervous. Later, you may use the emotion words on pages 34–36 to add to the list.

As you call out each word, and the students freeze, state that you see various differences in the students. For instance, if the word was "sad," you might say, *I see hands by the eyes because of crying, I see pouting lips, I see shoulders rounded over, and I see frowns.* Ask the students to look around and notice what other people look like when they are expressing emotions.

 Before you begin this activity, consider common physical traits of various emotions such as nervous, sad, mad, proud, etc. It will then be easier to describe these physical traits during the activity.

4 Next, have the students face the center of the room. Let them know that you will be telling a story using emotion words. Ask the students to become emotional statues after each emotion word is said.

1. You wake up and know it's your birthday. You are **happy**.

2. You go to school, and no one on the bus says, "Happy birthday." You are **sad**.

3. Then you go into class, and no one says anything about your birthday. You are **mad**.

4. You are called to the principal's office. You are **nervous**.

5. You see your parents through the window, and you wonder if you are in trouble. You are **scared**.

6. You walk in, see a cake with candles lit up, and "Happy Birthday" written on it. You are **surprised**.

7. And then you are **relieved**.

8. And **happy**.

As a lesson extension, have the students make up their own story using different emotion words.

5 The next step uses sentences without the emotion words. For instance, "You are called to the principal's office." The purpose is to show, and explain, that sometimes people react differently to similar situations. Tell the students that they should freeze at the end of each sentence in a manner that shows *their* feeling about the situation you just described. One might think that everyone would express some variation of nervousness or fear about being called to the principal's office. However, some people like to visit the principal and might show physical expressions of being happy. When the students freeze, describe the different emotional states that you see; some people are smiling and looking happy, some people have rounded shoulders and look sad, some people look nervous and are biting their fingernails.

Sample Scenarios

- You wake up and it is raining.
- Your classmates won't let you play with them at recess.
- You have the lead role, and today is the day of the play.
- You were called an insulting name.
- School is cut short because of bad weather, right before you were going to take a test.
- You hear there is a substitute teacher for art class.
- One of your friends says really mean things about your mother.
- Your parents are thinking about adopting a new baby.
- Someone started telling lies and rumors about you.
- The weather forecast calls for snow.
- Bigger students keep tripping you in the halls and always say it's an accident.

Final Thoughts

Recognizing physical cues of emotions, in one's self or others, is difficult for some children. While it might be easy for one child to recognize what emotion another is experiencing, it may not be obvious to another child. Ongoing refreshers of the emotional statues activity are helpful, fun ways to gain this important skill.

After the initial explanation of emotional statues, this activity may be played in short spurts with previously used as well as new emotion words (also used for spelling and vocabulary). Emotional statues may be done during morning meetings, indoor recess, and short breaks during long lessons when students need to be physical for a few moments.

STATISTICS AND STUDIES

- Program evaluation results have shown that schools where students are involved in programs designed to increase empathy and create "caring communities" have higher scores than comparison schools on measures of higher-order reading comprehension. (Kohn, 1991)
- Many people believe that bullies act tough in order to hide feelings of insecurity and self-loathing, while, in fact, bullies tend to be confident, with high self-esteem. (Nansel, et al., 2001)

- Bullies are generally physically aggressive, with pro-violence attitudes, and are typically hot-tempered, easily angered, and impulsive, with a low tolerance for frustration. Bullies have a strong need to dominate others and usually have little empathy for their targets. Male bullies are often physically bigger and stronger than their peers. (Olweus, 1993)

- Bullies tend to get in trouble more often, and to dislike and do more poorly in school, than teens who do not bully others. They are also more likely to fight, drink, and smoke than their peers. (Nansel, et al., 2001)

- Children who were exposed to violence in the home engaged in higher levels of physical bullying than youngsters who were not witnesses to such behavior, say researchers from the University of Washington and Indiana University. (Schwartz, 2006)

- "... some teenagers not only bully others but are also the targets of bullies themselves. Like other bullies, they tend to do poorly in school and engage in a number of problem behaviors. They also tend to be socially isolated, with few friends and poor relationships with their classmates." (Nansel, et al., 2001)

Unit Test
Chapters 1, 2, 3

Define bullying.

_____

_____

_____

List three types of bullying.

_____

_____

_____

List three examples of respectful behavior.

_____

_____

_____

What are the four ground rules?
I will not hurt . . .

_____

_____

_____

_____

The following are five steps of problem solving and conflict resolution. Using the numbers 1, 2, 3, 4, and 5, list the proper order.

_____ Decide Plan "A"

_____ Weigh the "Pros" and "Cons" of each idea

_____ Brainstorm Ideas

_____ Define the Problem or Conflict

_____ Decide Backup Plan "B"

True or False:

_____ If you don't like someone, you don't have to treat them with respect.

_____ Calling another person hurtful names doesn't really hurt the other person.

_____ Brainstorming means coming up with many ideas to solve a problem

Multiple Choice (circle the correct answers):

1. An example of respect is:
    a. asking someone what type of help they would like
    b. taking your friend's pencil without asking for permission
    c. burping in someone's face

2. An example of violence is:
    a. buying someone flowers
    b. throwing a rock at someone on purpose
    c. giving someone a "Hi-5" for doing well on a test

3. An example of resolving a conflict respectfully is:
    a. yelling at someone
    b. finding a solution that both people agree upon
    c. telling some kids they are too young to offer ideas

Describe what a person who is sad looks like.

_____

_____

Describe what a person who is angry looks like.

_____

_____

Describe what a person who is happy looks like.

_____

_____

Emotional Control and Anger Management

4

> *When angry, take a lesson from modern science: Always count down before blasting off.*
>
> —Anonymous

Pleasant or unpleasant, emotions are part of life. When they are pleasant, life is enjoyable; when they are unpleasant, life is challenging. To enjoy life and get along in society, each of us must manage the emotions we experience. Otherwise, emotions will take over and negatively influence how we think, behave, and lead our lives.

The activities in this section will help students recognize the physical cues of intense emotions and learn self-calming techniques so they may make acceptable choices when expressing feelings. An additional benefit to these lessons is that they reemphasize the qualities needed in empathy—how to recognize body language to determine how to act and react toward others.

As most elementary-age students are familiar with the emotion of anger, we focus on anger to teach emotional control. Review the emotion word list on pages 34–36 for other emotions that may also benefit from the following lessons.

GUIDED VISUALIZATIONS AND ANGER MONSTER POSTER

These activities help students identify and recognize the physical cues that indicate they are experiencing anger. Physical cues are specific areas of the body that are activated when there is intense emotion; these cues represent an emotional change from how a person feels during calm times. Examples of physical cues include tight fists or clenched teeth. When students become aware of their physical cues, they can learn how to address their emotions in a manner that is healthy, calming, and productive.

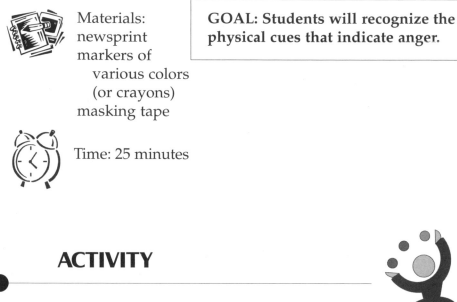

Materials:
newsprint
markers of
various colors
(or crayons)
masking tape

Time: 25 minutes

GOAL: Students will recognize the physical cues that indicate anger.

ACTIVITY

1 Explain to the students that they will be doing an anger memory exercise that will take about one to two minutes. Ask the students to close their eyes so they can focus on the exercise and avoid distraction. You will be guiding them to remember a time when they experienced anger; remembering where they were and the circumstances.

As you verbally guide your students to remember the situation that created the anger, ask them to be conscious of changes in how their bodies feel. Ask them to be aware of any tension in their hands, feet, or face, the feeling in their stomach, how fast they are breathing, and how fast their heart is beating.

! For some students, closing their eyes in a group situation brings up trust issues and causes them discomfort. Allow these students to keep their eyes open. Although you are requesting they close their eyes, don't force the issue. The allure of peeking will be great for some students, too. Allow this as well.

The following is an example of a guided visualization, but feel free to improvise. Begin with a medium pace and neutral tone of voice.

Suggested Script:

Close your eyes and think about a time when you were really feeling angry. What made you feel this way? What was happening that made you feel angry? Who was there when you were feeling angry?

Think about the things that made you angry. When you were feeling angry, what did your body feel like? How did your feet feel? What were your legs doing when you were feeling this powerful emotion? How did your stomach feel? Was it tight or loose? Think about your chest when you were angry. What was that like? How was your breathing? What was your heartbeat like?

When you were feeling angry, what were your hands like? What did they want to do? How about your arms and back? What about your face and head? What did the muscles feel like there? What were your eyes, nose, and mouth doing when you were experiencing this anger?

Pause for a few seconds.

I want you to remember these feelings and when you are ready, slowly open your eyes. Take a slow, deep breath.

2 Ask volunteers what they experienced in their body. Write two or three of these responses on the board. Some students will want to tell you what they were angry about. Remind them that you are not asking them what it is they were angry at, but the changes they became aware of throughout their body. Ask the rest of the students to remember the changes they felt during the exercise, but state that before you go any further in the lesson, you will help them get rid of any anger or tension they may still be experiencing with another visualization.

3 Ask the students to close their eyes again. In a soothing voice and pace, say . . .

Suggested Script:

It's a beautiful day. The weather is perfect. You are with people you like and who like you. Everyone is getting along, laughing, joking, and having a good time together. You are feeling really comfortable. You look and see your favorite drink. You take a sip. It tastes delicious and feels really refreshing. You are having a really great day and feeling good. There is no better place to be; you are calm and your breathing is slow, deep, and comforting. When you are ready, open your eyes.

This visualization teaches the students to use a self-calming technique when experiencing unpleasant emotions.

Remember to role model deep, slow breathing and let the sound of your soft breathing and that of the class continue for a short time.

An extra benefit of this exercise is how it shows the power of the mind. In the first exercise, the students remembered back to a time when they experienced being angry and even though it was only a mental exercise, some may have really felt how the anger caused physical changes in their body. Then they used their mind to create a peaceful place and feeling. Many will experience a physical calming during this visualization. Express to the students the value of knowing they have the potential to control the way their mind works, especially when they are having negative thoughts.

Some students may have a difficult time visualizing. Remind all the students that some people can really imagine themselves in another place during a visualization exercise, some students can "just kind of imagine it," and other students have a very difficult time really imagining being in a different place and time. Remind them that the most important part is to be willing to imagine. However it works for each person is OK.

Anger Monster Poster

4 Create a space on the floor large enough for you to unroll a sheet of newsprint (or equivalent) that is a little longer than your average student. There should also be enough space for all the students to comfortably gather around you and the newsprint. Ask for a volunteer who would be willing to have their body outlined with a crayon or marker.

Have the volunteer lay on the paper face up, with arms and legs stretched out comfortably, but still on the paper. Also make sure the fingers are outstretched. Use a marker to outline the body, making sure to trace each finger, the roundness of the shoulders, and the feet (with shoes on) laid out to the sides.

After drawing a complete outline, have the student carefully slide off the paper. The outline represents an average human body, and it could be anyone.

Figure 4.1

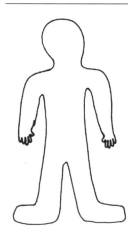

Let the volunteer student know *in advance* that you will be drawing on the poster and making it look VERY different. Tell the class that although you are using the student to create an outline, the outline is not representative of that student—it is just an outline of a human body.

Just as you had requested earlier, ask the students where in their body they felt physical changes when they were experiencing anger in the visualization. Responses should include answers that were stated earlier and written on the board. Now, as they say, "I wanted to punch," or, "My stomach felt funny," use colored markers to show each physical change on the paper outline. You can draw the hands as fists instead of relaxed and spread out. To show the stomach feeling funny you can draw butterflies or knots.

Ask prompting questions such as, "How did your eyes look or feel?" or, "Did your breathing change when you became angry?" Draw at least ten to twelve representations of the answers to these questions.

Changes in the poster should include some or all of the following:

- hair standing on end
- eyes red and beady
- eyebrows angled
- teeth clenched
- mouth tight
- fast, heavy breathing
- heart beating fast
- red face
- feet stomping
- knots or butterflies in stomach
- bridge of nose scrunched
- tense back and shoulders
- cloudy thinking

Artistic ability is not needed for this exercise; just do the best you can and do it fairly quickly. You can also write out words such as "fist," "stomach tight," "headache," "cloudy thinking," etc.

Figure 4.2

As you finish creating the Anger Monster, state that these changes in specific areas of the body are physical cues that a person is feeling anger. Recognizing these cues allows us to respond to the emotions, and the issue causing the emotions, in a healthy, rational manner.

Emotional statues also help students to become more aware of how to read the body language of others. Explain that if they see someone else showing signs of increasing agitation, it is a signal that the other person is losing control.

5 When you have finished creating the Anger Monster, roll up the poster and ask the students to go back to their seats. In dramatic style, tell the students that what they are about to see is what *they* said happens to them when they begin to experience intense anger. Unroll the paper and use the tape to hang up the poster. Explain that the poster reflects an Anger Monster. It is what some people look like when they have lost control of themselves and are in a rage.

Say, *If you are aware of your own feelings and body, or if you watch another when they are getting very angry, you can notice the change from calm to intense.*

Explain that you will now show how most people progress through anger with escalating physical responses. Ask the students to watch for your physical changes as you transition from normal teacher to Anger Monster.

Begin with your normal facial expression and slowly furrow your brow. Then clench your teeth, squint your eyes, and have your eyebrows angle down. Square up and tighten your shoulders. Have your hands turn into fists and follow with a subtle, but recognizable shaking in your arms. Begin to stomp around the room, grunting like an animal and threatening to turn over desks. Add drama by yelling, to no one in particular, statements such as, *I hate this place! No one is fair!* and, *This is stupid!* Be dramatic but remember not to scare your students. If you do this well, the students will laugh and learn.

Discuss your demonstration with the class, clarifying how angry people who are losing or have lost control look.

Suggested Script:

> *It is not the feeling of anger that is the problem. The problem is when you look and behave like this, you are losing or have lost control. The goal is to recognize physical cues before losing emotional and/or physical control. When you realize that your hands are turning into fists, or teeth are clenching, or recognize a change, it is a signal that you are experiencing anger and may lose control, may break the ground rules, or make matters worse.*
>
> *These physical cues will be different for everyone. Each of you has to discover your own cues so you can make good choices to either calm down or release your built up energy in a healthy, acceptable way.*

6 Have everyone stand up. Ask the students to each become an emotional statue of anger. Once again, ask them to be aware of the cues that indicate their body is experiencing anger. Finish this exercise by having the students do emotional statues of "relaxed" and "happy" to make sure they are left with bodies that are not experiencing anger.

Final Thoughts

Intense emotions other than anger also cause physical reactions. For instance, some people, when they are nervous, pick at their skin or pull their hair. Variations of these activities may be used to help students discover cues and unhealthy habits that are attributed to other emotions. Helping students become aware of the connection between their emotions and their mental and physical manifestations can facilitate replacing negative habits with healthy choices.

FEELING CLOUDS AND CHARADES— EXPRESSING FEELINGS IN PRO-SOCIAL WAYS

The visualization and Anger Monster activity are designed to help students discover cues to their emotional state. During the Ground Rules lesson (page 12), the students were taught what they *may not* do when they experience intense emotion. Now we have to teach them what they *may* do when they experience intense emotion. The Feeling Clouds and Charades game offers students strategies to calm their mind and body so they may address their emotions in a productive manner.

Materials per student:
8½ × 11 paper
pencil

GOAL: Students will practice strategies that help them calm down when angry.

Time: 30 minutes

ACTIVITY

1 Explain to the students that each individual has to learn how to recognize their emotions and still maintain calm, rational behavior.

Suggested Script:

Anger won't go away if we try to repress it, hold it back, or "stuff it down." Anger is an unpleasant feeling, but it won't go away just because you try to ignore it. Ignoring anger builds up a lot of pressure inside your mind and body, which can be very unhealthy. The pressure may grow and grow until you say or do things that make the situation worse. Or, the pressure may grow and instead of blowing outward, it goes inward. Sometimes, when that happens, people get headaches, stomachaches, depressed, or skin problems.

To avoid these problems, we have to feel the anger and still *make good choices. Everyone is allowed to have their feelings, but they still have to be responsible for their behavior. When we feel angry, we have to learn how to calm down so that we can make good choices. Making good choices helps lessen uncomfortable feelings and replace them with more pleasant feelings.*

Some calming strategies include taking slow, deep breaths; taking a walk; writing in a journal; listening to soft music; or some other activity that helps get back a feeling of self-control.

Some people calm down by releasing the energy of their anger through physical activity. Anger creates a lot of energy for some people. This type of person needs to release the energy that has been building or has built up, or they may find themself in an uncontrollable rage. They have *to do something physical to release the energy so they can calm down. This type of person might release physical energy by going for a run, exercising, playing the drums, throwing a ball, or another similar energy-releasing activity. This type of person needs to release energy, calm down, and regain self-control so they can address the issue that caused their anger.*

Solicit two or three other ideas from students on how to release energy appropriately.

2 Explain that to help each person consider what style works best for them, everyone will make a "Feeling Cloud." Hand out a white piece of paper to each student. Draw a cloud on your black/white board—an odd shaped, squiggly line circle (See Figure 4.3). Within the cloud, write, "When I feel angry I can _____, _____, or _____." Ask the students to make a similar drawing on their paper.

People who manage their emotions resolve conflicts peacefully and interact with others respectfully.

Figure 4.3

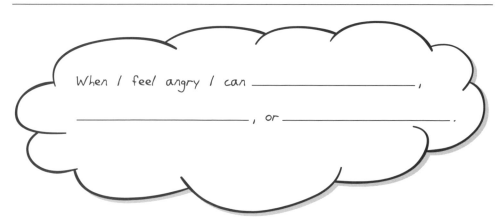

When I feel angry I can _____, _____, or _____.

3 Ask the students to think of at least three things they can do to help themselves calm down and/or release energy. Have the students write ideas that they know or think would work for them. Ask the students not to show each other their Feeling Clouds because they will be using them later. Suggestions may include:

baking	lifting weights	stacking wood
basketball	listening to music	swimming
dancing	lying down	taking a shower or
deep breathing	meditating	bath
drawing	painting	talking to a friend
exercise	playing an instrument	throwing a ball
favorite hobby	playing with pets	video games
gardening	practicing golf	visualizing
golfing	reading	walking
gymnastics	running	watching TV
hitting a punching bag	sculpting with clay	writing in a journal
kicking a ball	sewing or knitting	

! Some students might suggest energy releasing ideas such as target practice or working with power tools—activities that may be dangerous. Explain that target practice or working with power tools is generally acceptable, but not when you are angry. When feeling angry, having a weapon in your hands or using a powerful tool, no matter how old you are, is not a good idea. Acknowledge the need for adults to follow the same rules, too. For instance, you might say that when you are angry, you know it is not a good idea to drive a car. Both adults and children need to find safe alternatives to release their anger until they are calm.

Charades

4 Explain that Charades is a game where a person acts out, or pantomimes, thoughts, emotions, and feelings using only physical gestures—no words or sounds. For this activity, the students will act out what it is they do, or want to do, when they need to calm down. The other students have to guess what it is they are doing. Each student will use the Feeling Cloud activity to determine what they will act out.

Demonstrate how the activity is played; do something simple, like walking around the room as if you are outside taking a walk, and have the students guess what you are doing. Even though it should be easy for the students to guess what you are doing, most students enjoy the game quite a bit.

 The students will then take turns acting out their choices and the other students will guess what it is they are doing. Call several student volunteers up individually and have them whisper in your ear—for approval—what action they will act out or have them carry up their feeling cloud and point to their choice.

! Before a student pantomimes their calming technique, make sure it is an appropriate choice.

Final Thoughts

Some students will say they like to listen to music, watch TV or a movie, or play video games when they are very angry. This is an opportunity to reinforce their calming strategies and help refine their choices. Discuss what types of movies, music, or videos help them calm down. Compare and contrast the way louder, faster music and action movies make the students feel as opposed to more soothing choices of softer rock, jazz, or classical music, or comedies and light-hearted movies. Discuss which choices might be more effective in calming down emotions, instead of maintaining tension. In regard to computer or video games, suggest students choose video games that are nonviolent such as sports, logic, or art games and save the more violent games for a time when they are not feeling such strong emotions. Your words might not immediately change the opinion of those students who really like violent videos or movies, but the thought is an important one to introduce.

Lesson Extension

Mood Music

To effectively express how calming music can help sooth the mind, try the following activity. Hand out a sheet of paper and a crayon or marker to each student. Explain to the students that you will play some music and they are to close their eyes and draw on the paper in a free-flow manner—letting the feeling of the music dictate where the marker goes without consciously creating any particular type of drawing.

Begin by playing a twenty- to thirty-second sample of intense rock music to inspire the drawings. Then have the students turn over the paper. Play a sample of soft, soothing music and again have the students draw in free-flow style to this music.

Finally, have the students open their eyes and contrast the drawings that were inspired from the two different styles of music. Expect that the rock music side will have angular shapes and the softer music side will have more gentle swirls. This activity vividly shows how music can affect a mood.

DEEP BREATHING AND POSITIVE AFFIRMATIONS

When a person is expressing excitement or agitation beyond a reasonable measure, people will often say, "Calm down," "Take a deep breath," or suggest counting to ten. The behavioral expectation is to move to a calmer state, but transitioning from an excited state to a calm state can be difficult. It's a skill that has to be taught and practiced.

The strategy of taking ten slow, deep breaths to calm the mind and body may sound easy, but children must be taught the details of using this strategy. Without clear instruction and practice, many children will find themselves rapidly taking many shallow breaths, which will actually increase their agitation.

The following activities will teach students how to breathe deeply as an effective strategy to remain calm or regain composure in highly emotional situations. We will also teach the use of positive affirmations. Affirmations, or self-talk, can influence the way a person thinks and the actions one may take.

For some, it may be common sense that a deep breathing exercise needs to be slow and methodical to regain composure; others need to be taught the specifics of how to use the strategy effectively.

 Materials: none

> **GOAL: Students will learn how to take slow, deep breaths and use affirmations as a self-calming technique.**

 Time: 10 minutes

ACTIVITY

1 Suggested Script:

Two techniques to calm down, which everyone can use, are deep breathing and positive affirmations. Deep breathing can help calm your mind and body. It's an especially good skill to have if you aren't able to do one of your other, more physical or movement-oriented calming techniques.

As we learned, when we get angry or have other intense emotions, our muscles get tense, our breathing can get short and rapid, and our hearts may race. When we are dealing with those issues, it is difficult to think clearly and make good decisions. By purposely choosing to take slow, deep breaths we can get our mind and body back to a calm state. Positive affirmations, or positive self-talk, may also influence the way we think and the actions we take. We remind ourselves of our abilities, the type of people we want to be, and how we want to act.

Deep breathing and positive affirmations will help focus your body and mind to act, and react, in a way that is healthy and respectful to yourself and to those around you. They are great tools to use, either as your first choice to help calm you down, or as a back-up plan in case your first choice doesn't work.

The sound of the inhales and exhales of deep breathing should be quite soft. Point this out to your students.

2 Demonstrate deep breathing and positive affirmations by sitting in a chair, with your back straight, shoulders back, and head up. (This style of sitting extends your abdomen and chest so that it is easier to expand your inhalations.) Place your hands in front of you, on your lap, or on your desk. Ideally, it is preferable to close your eyes to limit distractions, but do so only if you are comfortable and it is appropriate while working with your students. Take a deep breath in, preferably through your nose, hold the breath for one to two seconds and then let it out quietly, through your mouth. Do this two or three times. Finally, take a deep breath and on the exhale, state a positive affirmation, such as, *"I am calm,"* or, *"I am relaxed."*

3 Before having the students imitate you, demonstrate how to do the exercise *incorrectly*. Tell the students that when people talk about trying to calm down by taking deep breaths or counting to ten, they do not mean breathing or counting very fast. Show the students the wrong way to breathe deeply with ten quick and dramatic inhales and exhales and fast counting. If you do this effectively, you should get a laugh from your students.

4 Lead the class in the proper technique of the exercise. Show the students how to sit in a comfortable position; either in a chair with feet on or toward the floor and hands on their lap, or by sitting crossed-legged on the floor with hands on lap. There is no one right way to sit in a relaxed manner; think of these positions as a suggestion, not a rule. Keeping eyes closed limits distractions and helps focus, but it's OK if a student prefers to keep their eyes open. Show an example of how to take a slow, deep, calming breath by breathing in through the nose, holding the breath for one to two seconds and then letting the breath out slowly through the mouth (if a cold or allergies prevent inhaling through the nose, breathing through the mouth is acceptable). Have the students follow your lead and together practice this exercise between seven and ten times. State that if done correctly, others should barely hear their inhales or exhales.

On each proceeding inhale, guide the students to hold their breath a bit longer. Consider adding the following instructions in a soft voice to help students become more aware of their physical state and to relax further:

- *Imagine your breath expanding your lungs.*
- *Feel the air filling your chest—expanding your chest as if it were a balloon.*
- *Feel your shoulders spread out and back as you take deeper breaths.*

These instructions help students focus on what they should be imagining so that the exercise is more effective.

5 After the students are proficient and comfortable with deep breathing, add affirmations to the deep breathing exercise. Affirmations are positive statements declared to be true.

Instruct the students to breathe along with you and to repeat the affirmations that you will be stating as they exhale. Using a soothing voice, say and do the following:

1. *Breathe in through your nose.* You and the students quietly inhale. Hold the breath for one or two seconds.

2. Exhale and say, *I am relaxed.* The students exhale, saying, "I am relaxed."

Note that all statements are in the present tense. This will help students focus on the desired present state of being, not a future goal. In other words, "I am calm," not, "I will be calm."

Suggested affirmations:

- I am calm.
- I am relaxed.
- My breathing is slow and steady.
- I am peaceful and respectful even when angry.
- I can solve my problems peacefully.
- I am a respectful person.
- I am a good friend.
- I can be strong without being aggressive.
- I deserve to be treated with respect.
- I treat others respectfully.
- I express my thoughts respectfully.

When including affirmations along with deep breathing, you can either state the same affirmations repeatedly or vary them. The best way is the way that works for you and your students.

Lesson Extension

A great way to show how effectively these exercises calm the body and mind is to lead the students in a round of jumping jacks *immediately* followed by the deep breathing exercise. Have your students do enough jumping jacks to increase their heart rates and breathing. When they first begin the deep breathing exercise, it will be difficult to hold their breath for one to two seconds. As they continue, their inhalations will get deeper and they will be able to control their breathing patterns. Ask them to be aware of the change in their heart rates, too. Add affirmations such as, "My breathing is slow and steady," and, "My heart is beating slowly."

As you continue to practice these skills with your students, you can add new and different affirmations. Better yet, have students come up with new affirmations. One group of students with whom we worked used this exercise before a test when students were feeling mighty anxious. One student volunteered, "I am great at math." It became a very popular affirmation.

Final Thoughts

Practice deep breathing and positive affirmations with your students on a regular basis. Consider using this calming strategy to help students transition from a high level activity such as recess to a low level activity such as academic instruction.

ABCD EXERCISE

(**A**wareness, **B**ack off and **B**reathe, **C**hoices, **D**o it)

Materials: none

GOAL: Students will use their self-calming techniques when they recognize that they are experiencing powerful emotions.

Time: 15 minutes

ACTIVITY

1 Suggested Script:

Now that we have learned to recognize our physical cues and how to calm down, we will practice these skills so that we will be ready when anger or other emotions arise. The goal is to be prepared to deal with strong feelings and maintain calm and reasonable thinking. We are going to learn and practice an exercise so that when our physical cues signal strong emotions, we can go into "calm down" mode.

2 Write the letters "A," "B," "C," and "D" on the board vertically (See Figure 4.4).

Figure 4.4

One by one, you will write out what word each letter represents. Do not write the explanation of each word, but discuss the concept behind each word before moving on to the next letter.

Suggested Script:

Awareness—*means becoming aware that a physical cue of strong feelings is activated, such as what was learned during the Emotional Statues and Anger Monster activities. For example, you might become aware that you are feeling angry because your hands have become clenched fists or you want to kick.*

Back off and Breathe—means taking a step back with one foot and taking a slow, deep breath in through the nose. This step back is used as a reminder to physically and emotionally back off from the situation to avoid reacting hastily. The deep breath helps to slow down the mind and body so that you can consider your next decision and make a wise choice.

Choices—means consider which choice you want to use to maintain calm behavior. Choices may include taking a walk, kicking a soccer ball, writing in a journal, or deep breathing and positive affirmations. A good physical reminder to remember this step is to touch your head with your index finger, which will remind you to think of your choices.

Do it—means doing the activity that will help you maintain calm. Coming up with a great idea is only as good as carrying out the idea. Using the charades game technique, you will stand in place and pantomime your choice for calming down or releasing energy. It is not practical to have everyone actually go for a run, bake cookies, or play the drums, so you will act out the choice in place.

3 Demonstrate the ABCD exercise by performing each step in order:

Awareness—"I am aware that I am getting angry" (show your emotional statue of anger).

Back off and **B**reathe—show how you take one step back and take a deep breath (in through the nose, out through the mouth).

Choices—place your index finger on your head (physical reminder). Note that you don't actually do the activity at this point; it is just a moment to consider a good choice.

Do it—in place, pantomime the action you chose as your example when you discussed the feeling clouds and played the charades game (e.g., walking, running, knitting, talking on the phone, lifting weights).

Remember that you are leading by example. Not only are you instructing, you also need to do the exercise.

4 Practice the exercise with the students. Ask the students to stand up. The area around the students should be clear. If you have available space, have the students stand in a circle so they can see each other. Let the students know they should do the steps along with you, using their own emotional statues and activity choices.

1. Say, "***A**—be aware that you are becoming very angry.*" Show your angry emotional statue, which the students should also do.

2. Say, "***B**—back off and breathe.*" You and the students should take one step back while quietly inhaling and exhaling.

3. Say, "***C**—consider your choices.*" Put your finger on your head, which the students should also do.

4. Say, "***D**—do it.*" As you stand in place, pantomime your choice, while the students pantomime their choices.

As the students are all pantomiming their choices, state the different choices you see the students performing, such as walking, kicking a soccer ball, dancing, talking on the phone. This reinforces good choices and helps students consider other good choices.

5 Students usually understand how to do the exercise after one or two rounds. After the students demonstrate that they are proficient with the exercise, prepare the students for adding a new step to the process.

Explain that removing yourself from a situation where you are likely to break one of the ground rules or overreact is a good first choice. This might mean walking away from someone who says something insulting to you, away from a computer that is frustrating you, or away from your dog who made a mess on your bedroom floor for the third time in a week. When you include removing yourself from a situation as part of practicing the ABCD exercise, you are increasing the odds that students will remove themselves or use a calming action when they experience anger or other strong emotions.

For this round of the exercise, when you say, "D—do it," have your students walk to a neutral, empty part of the classroom, within your eyesight, to act out their pantomime. They will have until the count of five to *walk* to that spot. Each student should be at least an arm's distance from another person or thing. When you say, "five," each student should then pantomime their choice.

6 Before concluding the ABCD exercise session, go through the sequence one final time. During this last time, state to the students that on the final round, the "C" choice for everyone will be taking deep breaths and making positive affirmations.

Suggested Script:

> *As discussed during the conflict resolution lesson, it is important to always have a back-up plan, or Plan "B," in case you can't perform your first choice. For instance, if someone likes to go for a run when they get upset, but finds themselves in the backseat of the car and their brother or sister is really annoying them, it's unlikely the driver will stop to let the person go running on the side of a highway. Therefore, a good Plan "B" calming idea is deep breathing with silent affirmations.*
>
> *It is important to practice deep breathing with silent affirmations because you can do it almost anywhere and anytime; in the back*

Provide opportunities for the students to watch other students do this exercise so they can see choices others might make, which may increase their own repertoire of appropriate choices.

Practice this exercise with other emotions. For instance, try "A"—awareness of being "nervous."

seat of a car, in the classroom, in the living room, on a ball field, in a bathroom, wherever. Other people don't even have to know you are doing it. If done correctly, you can turn your head away from the person who is bothering you and your breathing should be so quiet that even the person right next to you can't hear you.

For the final ABCD sequence, when it comes time to "D—do it," have the students sit right down on the floor or in a nearby vacant chair. Then lead a deep breathing exercise as described in the deep breathing lesson on page 55.

Have the students take five to ten deep breaths and add affirmations as desired.

Final Thoughts

Practicing the ABCD exercise is similar to practicing a fire drill. Fire drills are practiced when there is no danger. You don't wait until smoke is billowing and flames are licking at your feet to practice how to get everyone out of the building safely. By practicing when there is no danger, there is a better chance everyone will know what they should do if there is danger and everyone is really scared. Likewise, the ABCD exercise is practiced when we are emotionally and intellectually in control. Then, if we find ourselves losing control, we are better prepared to make good decisions and regain or maintain self-control.

STATISTICS AND STUDIES

- "Being bullied is not just an unpleasant rite of passage through childhood," said Duane Alexander, MD, director of the National Institute of Child Health and Human Development. "It's a public health problem that merits attention. People who were bullied as children are more likely to suffer from depression and low self-esteem, well into adulthood, and the bullies themselves are more likely to engage in criminal behavior later in life." (National Institutes of Health, 2001)
- Direct, physical bullying increases in elementary school, peaks in middle school, and declines in high school. (Garrett, 2003)
- Sixty percent of those characterized as bullies in grades 6–9 had at least one criminal conviction by age twenty-four. (Olweus, 1993)

Teaching Assertiveness 5

> *Assertiveness is standing up for yourself without stepping on others.*
> —Elizabeth Janice

Assertiveness is the ability to honestly express opinions, feelings, and rights in a manner that doesn't infringe on the rights of others. It is the middle ground between being aggressive and passive. Teaching students how to communicate assertively can minimize bullying, lead to self-respect, and increase respect from others.

Assertiveness training teaches aggressive students how to get their needs met in a pro-social manner that is not abusive. Assertiveness training also teaches passive people specific behaviors that will help them express their wants and needs in a manner that will lead to greater self-confidence.

Later, in Chapter 6, Responding to a Bully, and Chapter 7, The Power of Bystanders, we will apply assertive communication techniques as an effective tool to stop a bullying episode.

TEACHING ASSERTIVE COMMUNICATION

This lesson is designed to teach assertive communication and how it compares to other styles of communication: aggressive, passive, and passive-aggressive. This lesson is much more effective, and more fun, if you use an expressive and dramatic teaching style to describe these different styles of communication.

Materials per student:
paper
pencil

GOAL: Students will learn the definition of assertiveness and the qualities it takes to express themselves in an assertive manner.

 Time: 25 minutes

ACTIVITY

1 Write the word "assertive" on the board.

Suggested Script:

> Assertiveness is the type of communication you use when you really want the other person to take you seriously. You are showing self-respect by giving yourself an opportunity to express your thoughts and feelings. You express respect to the other person by speaking in a manner that considers their thoughts and feelings. You also increase the chance that others will respect your thoughts and feelings on a regular basis.
>
> To communicate assertively you have to be aware of the following qualities:
> - **A calm demeanor**
> - **Body language**—posture displaying a stillness and strength
> - **Eye contact**—but do not "stare down"
> - **A neutral tone of voice**—with depth—not too loud, too soft, whiny, or sarcastic
> - **Say what you want**—short and to the point

Fifty-five percent of communication is visual (body language, eye contact), 38 percent is vocal (pitch, speed, volume, tone of voice), and 7 percent is the actual words. (Gallo, 2007)

Using these qualities, demonstrate the following examples of assertive communication (or use your own examples).

1. "Thanks for dinner, Mrs. Mendoza, but I really don't like broccoli. I think I'll just eat the chicken and mashed potatoes."

2. "Please don't tease me about my haircut."

3. "It's not cool to talk about someone behind their back."

4. "Hey, Mom, I would really like to stay up a little later to finish watching this show. May I stay up an extra half hour?"

2 Have the students write "assertiveness" on their paper (See Figure 5.1). To the extent appropriate for your students, explain and discuss each of the following five qualities of assertive communication using the descriptions provided. As you explain each quality, write it on the board and have the students write it on their paper as shown in Figures 5.1, 5.2, 5.3, 5.4, and 5.5.

Figure 5.1

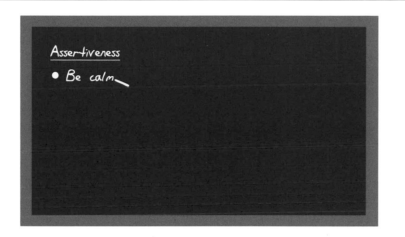

1. Be Calm

Suggested Script:

> *Expressing thoughts and feelings can be hard. You may be uncomfortable with the person you need to speak to, how that person might react, or about the topic. You may also be dealing with emotions such as fear, anger, embarrassment, uncertainty, or intimidation.*
>
> *You have a better chance of getting someone to listen to you if you are calm when you are talking to them. You can show that you are calm through your body language, eye contact, tone of voice, and the words you choose.*

2. Body Language

Figure 5.2

Suggested Script:

Calm body language will increase the chance that the listener will focus on your words, not your physical movements. When communicating assertively, you should stand still. There should be no extra movements in your head, body, or even eyes.

Demonstrate Body Language

Physically and verbally demonstrating the "Do's" and "Don'ts" of assertive communication will increase the students' understanding of the concepts.

WHAT NOT TO DO:

The WHAT NOT TO DO section is a good place to be dramatic and exaggerate to emphasize what should not be done.

- Bend over or toward the person in a threatening way.
- Shift your weight back and forth on your legs or hips (like a strange dance or like you really need to go to the bathroom, a.k.a. The Pee Dance).
- Fold your arms across your body.
- Rest your hands on your hips.
- Move your hands or head around.
- Stand as if you are a soldier at attention or stiff as a statue.

WHAT TO DO:
- Stand straight.
- Keep legs shoulder width apart.
- Hold head and back straight.
- Relax arms.

3. Eye contact

Figure 5.3

Folding your arms or resting your hands on your hips is not necessarily aggressive or rude. However, during a serious conversation, these poses can be misinterpreted and therefore it is not in the speaker's best interest to stand that way.

Suggested Script:

Making eye contact with the person you are talking to expresses confidence and lets the person know that you are talking directly to them. It also helps you to know if the other person is paying attention, if they understand what you are saying, and how they are feeling about what you are saying.

! In certain families and cultures, children are taught not to look into the eyes of an adult. Let those students know that you respect and value their culture, but in school the expectation is that you will make eye contact when speaking to a peer or to an adult.

Demonstrate Eye Contact

WHAT NOT TO DO:

- Stare, glare, attempt to intimidate or make the other person uncomfortable with too much eye contact; generally, seven to ten seconds at one time would be considered too long.
- Look at the ceiling or the floor; it will appear as if you are not interested in the other person or you are unsure of yourself.
- Make a lot of eye movement.
- Roll your eyes.

WHAT TO DO:
- Look into the eyes of the person with whom you are speaking.
- Look at the person you are talking to for about two or three seconds and then look slightly away for about one or two seconds. Repeat this rhythm, but do not be too methodical.
- Be aware of the other person's comfort level with eye contact. Try to adapt by increasing or decreasing eye contact to maintain mutual comfort.

4. Tone of Voice

Figure 5.4

Suggested Script:

Your tone of voice should be calm and controlled—not too fast, not too slow, not too loud, and not too soft. These qualities are the best chance for your words and feelings to be heard and respected.

Demonstrate Tone of Voice

WHAT NOT TO DO:
- Yell or scream.
- Speak too quickly.
- Talk so softly the listener has to struggle to hear you.
- Use a sarcastic tone—saying one thing but meaning another or the exact opposite.
- Mumble or whine.

WHAT TO DO:
- Speak loud enough so the person can hear you without struggling.
- Speak soft enough so that you are not overwhelming the listener by being too loud.

If a student has a difficult time looking into someone's eyes, instruct them to focus on an area of the face that is close to the eyes. For instance, focusing on the tip of the person's nose, bridge of the nose, the eyebrows, or the area right below the eyes can be a good place to focus.

If the speaker's tone distracts the listener, the words will not be heard.

- Keep your mouth and throat relatively relaxed (to avoid sounding strained or crackly).
- Use a medium speaking pace; not too fast, not too slow.

5. Words: Say What You Want

Sarcasm is ineffective when a person wants another to clearly understand what they are saying.

Figure 5.5

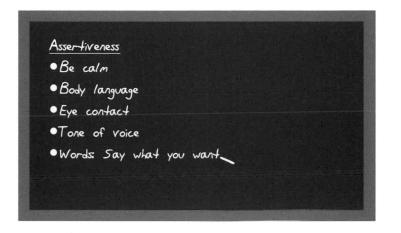

Suggested Script:

Say what you want—short in length and to the point. Too many words might cause the listener to stop listening. In addition, using mean or hurtful words will cause the listener to stop listening to you. Using polite language increases the chance that the person you are talking to will focus on what you are saying.

 If you discover that your students use words that do not reflect the values of your school or classroom, you will need to specifically teach which words are acceptable and which words are not.

Saying What You Want

WHAT NOT TO DO:
- Talk too much.
- Swear or curse.
- Insult.
- Put down or belittle the other person.
- Threaten or intimidate.
- Be sarcastic.
- Use words that hurt.

WHAT TO DO:
- Say exactly what you mean or what you want.
- Keep your statements short and to the point.
- Use words and phrases such as, "in my opinion," "I feel . . ." and "I would appreciate . . ."

Other Styles of Communication

3 Before practicing the skills of assertive communication, discuss the other styles of communication: aggressive, passive, and passive-aggressive, all of which have advantages and disadvantages. It is important to discuss these other styles of communication to clarify how assertive communication is more effective compared with these styles with which the students may be more familiar.

Aggressive Communication

Suggested Script:

> *Assertive communication is an effective and respectful style of communication, but many people choose other ways to communicate their thoughts and feelings. Some people use yelling and threatening, others use moping and hoping, and some pretend friendliness but then purposely mistreat you.*
>
> *An aggressive style of communication is used by some when they have strong feelings or want others to pay attention to them. They will often yell, scream, threaten, intimidate, name-call, or use curse and swear words.*
>
> *The advantage to this style is that it can work. People who communicate aggressively sometimes get what they want. If the people they are talking to get scared and do what they say, the aggressive person learns that yelling and threatening works. Then they feel powerful, in control, and will continue to be aggressive.*
>
> *The disadvantage to communicating aggressively is that although it may work sometimes, it often causes the aggressive person more problems. Being aggressive will turn people off, cause the aggressive person to lose friends, and may get them into trouble. There are better ways a person can get what they want without hurting or scaring others.*

Demonstrate (be dramatic):
Act out examples of an aggressive person. Do this by:

- Positioning yourself in a defiant stance, using tense body language, glaring eyes, clenched mouth, and pointing a finger or shaking a fist.

- Telling someone to *"Shut up!"* (Do not say this too close to any student.)
- Grabbing someone's pencil or water bottle without permission.
- Saying, *"We're either playing my game or you can just go home!"*
- Making a fist and saying, *"Do that again and I'll smash you!"*
- Saying, *"We don't allow babies like you to play."*

Other examples of a person being aggressive include:

- Always telling other students what to do
- Taunting others by calling them names
- Threatening others

Passive Communication

Suggested Script:

A passive style of communication means accepting the way something is without protesting or objecting even when you disagree. Passive people give off the impression that they are giving permission or approval by not speaking up or taking action. Passive people like to avoid conflict and usually don't like to make decisions. Some passive people believe they will have more friends by always going along with others no matter what they truly feel or think. It is not passive if a person truly doesn't care about a situation.

The disadvantage of this style is that passive people take less control of their lives and allow others to take charge of what happens to them. Without expressing their thoughts and desires, they have to hope that others choose things that they also like.

Demonstrate:

Act out examples of a passive person.

- Stand still, looking somewhat neutral and quiet. Explain that a passive person often does not show emotion or offer other clues through their body language. Although sometimes, if you pay attention, you may notice they may look sad or upset.
- Meekly say, *"OK, if that's what everyone wants to do. I guess it's OK with me."*

Explain, *"It is OK if you really don't care what you do but passive people say, 'It's OK,' even when they really do care. If you really don't care, it should be stated in an assertive manner, not passively."* Clarify this point by stating the previous sentence assertively, and compare it to the way you stated it passively.

Passive-Aggressive Communication

Suggested Script:

Another style of communication is called passive-aggressive. People who are passive-aggressive don't express their thoughts and feelings in a direct way. They show their thoughts and feelings through aggressive behaviors in an indirect way.

An example of a passive-aggressive act is taking a book out of the library just to prevent the person you are angry at from being able to get the book. Other examples include making someone wait on purpose or destroying someone's property without the person knowing who did it. Starting a rumor or a lie about someone, without anyone knowing where the rumor started, is also a type of passive-aggressive communication.

The advantage of this type of communication is that a person can avoid directly expressing thoughts or feelings to another person. And there may be some satisfaction from causing trouble for people they are unhappy with.

The disadvantage is that passive-aggressive people do not speak up for themselves and don't get what they really want. Like aggressive people, passive-aggressive people may get in trouble when their aggressive actions are discovered.

Final Thoughts

Learning how to communicate assertively is vital in teaching students to express their thoughts and emotions appropriately, to resolve conflicts peacefully, and to develop and maintain healthy relationships. It is important to teach students the terms for other styles of communication, as they may be familiar with the style but not the terms. This knowledge should help them understand the full spectrum of choices in how people communicate and determine why assertive communication is in their own best interest.

HANDSHAKING—USING THE QUALITIES OF ASSERTIVENESS

Handshaking is a critical component of interpersonal relationships both socially and professionally. It is a skill your students will need throughout their lives. Understanding the basics of a respectful, proper handshake will help them understand how to express themselves assertively. In effect, an assertive, proper handshake represents a balance of power—not too hard and not too soft.

Materials:
none

GOAL: Students will learn how
to shake hands.

Time: 15 minutes

ACTIVITY

The Standard Handshake

Suggested Script:

A fun way to understand how to communicate assertively is practicing a proper handshake. Learning to shake hands properly will help you to remember the qualities of assertive communication.

When shaking someone's hand, you walk up to a person, stand about one and a half feet from the other person, extend your right arm at a slight angle across your body, toward the other person's right hand, and with your hand open, your palm facing left and your thumb pointing upward, grasp the other person's hand, squeeze a medium amount—not too hard or too soft—and give about two or three up and down shakes.

1 Demonstrate a Proper Handshake

Figure 5.6

Ask for a volunteer to join you in front of the class to demonstrate an assertive handshake. Begin the demonstration by standing about twelve to fifteen feet apart. Walk toward the volunteer, extend your right arm at a slight angle across the body—toward the other person's right hand—and with your hand open, your palm facing left and your thumb pointing upward, grasp the volunteer's hand and execute a proper handshake.

Articulating the conscious and detailed action that takes place during a proper handshake will be useful to inexperienced students.

---

2 Explain the details of a proper handshake.

Suggested Script:

> *Both people shake with their right hand, even if one or both are lefties. Of course, there are exceptions to this rule. If a person doesn't have a right hand, they will offer their left hand to shake. Usually the other person will then offer their left hand, although occasionally the handshaking is with one person's left hand and other person's right hand. Another reason a person will offer their left hand is because their right hand is injured. If this is the case, it is acceptable to offer the left hand and say, "I have an injured right hand."*

> *It is believed that handshaking originated as a gesture showing that the hand holds no weapon.*

Personal space—*During a proper handshake, the two people stand close enough to shake hands but distant enough to respect each other's personal space. The distance between the two people should be about a foot and a half.*

Eye contact—*The two people make eye contact for two to four seconds. Occasional eye contact will then continue for the conversation.*

Grasping hands—*A proper handshake has both people holding the other person's full hand. This means that the web between your thumb and index finger should intersect with the other person's web. The hand should be flat enough so your palms are touching. It is normal to shake, or pump, your hand two or three times. Sometimes hands don't always connect in just the right way and it is OK to just let it be when that happens.*

Words—*Whatever you say should be easily understood by the other person, such as, "Hello, nice to meet you," or, "Hey, good job today!" It is especially important to speak clearly when you state your own name during an introduction, such as, "My name is Dana." If you mumble or say your name too softly, the other person might get the impression that you are overly shy or embarrassed. It is your name, and you should express pride by stating it clearly.*

3 Improper Handshakes

Suggested Script:

Earlier we talked about aggressive, passive, and passive-aggressive communication. People can also shake hands aggressively, passively, or passive-aggressively.

I will over-dramatize the wrong way to shake hands to make the point clear. But don't worry, I won't hurt anyone or be too gross.

The Aggressive Handshake
Through their handshake, an aggressive person comes across as if they need to show they are physically strong. They squeeze a person's hand too tightly. They may even speak too loudly or stand too close.

Demonstrate the aggressive handshake

Figure 5.7

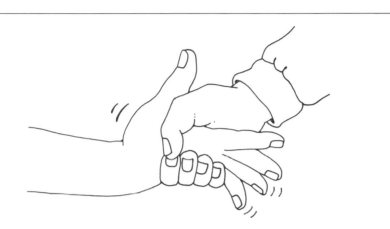

Ask for another volunteer to join you in front of the class. Begin by standing about twelve–fifteen feet apart. Walk toward the volunteer, but this time make a grand and overly dramatic, sweeping gesture with your arm and grab hold of their hand.

Continue to walk right into that person's personal space. Make believe you are squeezing the volunteer's hand VERY tightly, unconcerned about hurting their hand. Loudly say, *"Hi. My name is _____."* This is an aggressive handshake.

A variation of the aggressive handshake is called . . . the twisting handshake.
This style of handshaking starts out as a proper handshake, but then becomes aggressive by twisting the other person's hand and arm.

Demonstrate the twisting handshake

Figure 5.8

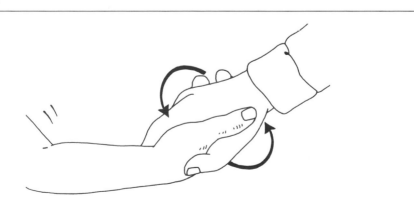

Demonstrate the twisting handshake by starting out with a respectful handshake but then twist the volunteer's arm. Over-dramatize this handshake to make the point, but be careful not to hurt the student.

Demonstrate the passive handshake

Figure 5.9

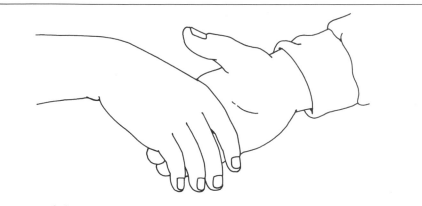

Suggested Script:

> *People who shake hands passively are thought of as being weak or lacking self-confidence. They squeeze the other person's hand too softly. They may speak too quietly or not at all, and they may not make eye contact.*

Demonstrate this type of handshake by, once again, standing about twelve to fifteen feet apart. Looking toward the ground, shuffle up to the other person and extend your right arm, angling toward the ground, as opposed to across your body. Place your hand in the other person's hand, but don't squeeze at all or just barely. Very softly say, *"My name is _____."*

Explain that sometimes people give passive handshakes for other reasons. *Some people, sometimes very big people, use a very soft handshake because they are overly concerned about being too aggressive and therefore shake hands very softly. They are not weak, passive, or lacking confidence; they have just not found the proper handshaking pressure that is good for both people.*

One style that appears passive but may not be is called the palm pinch.

Demonstrate the palm pinch

Figure 5.10

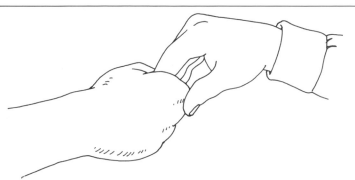

A palm pincher offers just two or three fingers to shake. Sometimes older women will use this type of handshake as it used to be the appropriate way for women to shake hands. However, this does not apply anymore.

Begin the demonstration by standing about twelve to fifteen feet apart. Walk toward the volunteer, extend your right arm at a slight angle across the body—toward the other person's right hand—and with your hand open, your palm facing downward and your thumb pointing to the left offer the volunteer two or three fingers to shake.

Passive-Aggressive Handshakes

Explain the following, but do not demonstrate (because it's disgusting).

Suggested Script:

A passive-aggressive handshake seems respectful and assertive but isn't. Here's an example of a passive-aggressive handshake. A person goes to shake someone's hand, however, before the hand is shaken, and without anyone seeing, the person spits on their own hand. The person who shakes the hand doesn't realize they now have spit on their hand. This is passive-aggressive because it appears as if it is respectful, but it is really aggressive. Another example is shaking someone's hand when you know that your hand is very dirty, or has not been recently washed and should have been, such as after using the toilet. It is passive-aggressive if you think the other person would not want to touch your hand but you fool them into doing it anyway.

4 Have the students practice handshaking with each other. Have them walk around the room and "introduce" themselves to the other students. Make sure all students participate.

5 Have the students form a circle. Explain that you will introduce yourself to each student, as if you were meeting for the first time. The students will be expected to shake your hand, introduce themselves, and say something like, "Hello," "Nice to meet you," or, "How are you?" In turn, you will give an appropriate response.

Remind the students that when it is their turn to shake hands, they should be assertive with their body language, eye contact, and tone of voice. Let the students know that if they give you a handshake that is too hard or too soft, or they are . . .

- slouching,
- dangling a foot off to the side,
- standing with one hip uneven with the other,
- not making eye contact, or
- not stating their name clearly,

. . . you will respectfully correct them and ask them to do it again. This is not meant to embarrass the person; it is about working on a skill that has to be practiced—like basketball or dancing.

Remember to compliment the students when they give a correct handshake, mentioning a positive quality of their handshake.

Hi-5s (A Variation on Handshaking)

Although shaking hands is a must-know skill in Western culture, most elementary age students do not shake hands with each other. It is more common that they slap hands. Therefore, another way to practice assertiveness is with Hi-5s—similar to the way athletes slap hands with each other during or after a game.

Suggested Script:

> *Hi-5s are similar to handshakes. In an assertive Hi-5, each person's slap of the hand is about equal in force to a person clapping. An aggressive Hi-5 is purposely slapping the other person's hand hard. A passive Hi-5 is one in which the other person hardly feels that you slapped their hand at all. An example of a passive-aggressive Hi-5 is spitting in your hand when the other person is not looking and then giving them what appears to be an assertive Hi-5.*
>
> Go around the room and have each student give you a Hi-5. If the student gives you a Hi-5 that is too hard or too soft, correct them and ask them to do it again.

Final Thoughts

Handshaking and Hi-5s are physical manifestations of assertive behavior and a respectful communication style. Make it a point to find reasons to shake your students' hands or to give them a Hi-5 during the day.

On another note, some physical contact between student and teacher may be misinterpreted. Some students, especially young students, like to give and get hugs from teachers they admire. Try using handshakes and Hi-5s as a means to express the closeness and bond they want to share. This also goes a long way in teaching these children appropriate personal boundaries.

RECOGNIZING ASSERTIVE, AGGRESSIVE, AND PASSIVE COMMUNICATION STYLES

To all my faults, my eyes are blind;
Mine are the sins I cannot find.
But your mistakes, I see a-plenty,
For them, my eyes are twenty-twenty.

—MINNIE BREAKSTONE YURIK (AMERICAN ENTERTAINER)

People notice what other people do that is incorrect, insincere, or hypocritical sooner than they will recognize those qualities in themselves. Young people are especially quick to pick up this incongruity if we don't role model the behavior we say we expect from them. This activity helps students to recognize and clarify behavior from an objective perspective and is a prelude to helping them recognize their own behavior and style of communication.

Materials:
three large pieces
   of paper; one with
   the word AGGRESSIVE
   written on it, one with
   ASSERTIVE on it, one
   with PASSIVE on it
tape

GOAL: Students will recognize different styles of communication.

Time: 20 minutes

ACTIVITY

1 For the following activity, you will need to create a large, open space that has room for the students to move about. You might want to move the desks and chairs off to the side.

If it is necessary to move furniture around the room, ask the students to help. Remind them, *before they begin to move things*, that respectful behavior means moving the desks without knocking things over, or bumping into people or desks. Also, they should lift the chairs and desks so that they don't scrape the floor or create a noise that might be disruptive to other classes. If some students do not follow these instructions appropriately, assertively remind or demonstrate how to move a desk and chair correctly.

Divide the room into three sections: On one side of the room you will tape up the PASSIVE sign. On the opposite side, tape up the AGGRESSIVE sign. In the middle of the room, tape up the ASSERTIVE sign, or lay the sign on the floor. To begin the activity, the students will be standing in the middle of the room—the "assertive" area.

You will read or role-play a scene. In each scene, there are three different ways to behave: assertively, passively, or aggressively. Begin this activity by describing a scene (see Scene 1) to the class. Act out the first possible response (see Scene 1-A) that will be an example of a communication style. Have students wait for you to say, "Go." When you say, "Go," they should walk slowly toward the sign they believe expresses how you behaved in the scene. Ask a few students to discuss what criteria they used to determine if your response was assertive, passive, or aggressive.

You will then present the same scenario, but during this second time, give the second response variation (see Scene 1-B). Again, ask the students to stand near the sign that expresses how you behaved in that role-play. Repeat the activity with the third response variation (see Scene 1-C). Repeat with Scene 2 and Scene 3.

 Suggested Script:

I will describe or act out a scene. In each of the following scenes, I will act either assertively, passively, or aggressively. Listen and watch, and when I say, "Go," walk slowly toward the sign you believe expresses how I behaved in the scene. We will then discuss how you determined your response.

3 **Role-Playing Scenarios to Determine Communication Style**

NOTE: For each scene use another adult or a student as the other person in the role-play.

Scene 1: Explain and act out the scene. *"Your brother or sister is on the computer and IMing. You need the computer to do a homework assignment, and it is getting late."*

    A. *"Get off the computer! All you are doing is fooling around. Hurry up!"*

    B. *"Excuse me. Would you please get off the computer for a little while so I can do my homework? Then you can have it back."*

    C. Just stand near your brother or sister and hope your sibling takes the hint.

Scene 2: Explain and act out the scene. *"Someone steps in front of you in line."*

    A. *"Excuse me. I was in line and you stepped in front of me."*

    B. Do not say anything, but cross your arms and pout.

    C. *"Hey, get out of here you idiot. I was here first!"* (Pantomime or make believe you are aggressively pushing your partner. Then move in front of the person.)

Scene 3: Explain and act out the scene. *"You are enjoying a TV show and your brother or sister comes in the room and wants to watch a different show."* (Note: This time there are two different types of assertive responses, A and D.)

    A. *"I'm enjoying this show, but it's over in 15 minutes and then you can watch whatever you want."*

    B. Sigh and say in a soft, somewhat defeated tone, *"Fine, watch whatever you want."*

    C. *"No way. Your show is stupid!"*

    D. *"Sure, here's the remote. I was just surfing anyway."*

Final Thoughts

Most elementary school students will quickly note the correct response in each scenario. However, you will have a percentage of students who will stand by the correct sign *only* because they are going along with the majority of the crowd. Going along with the crowd may be typical behavior for them. Others might be at the wrong sign because they truly are having difficulty discerning the difference between the styles or the definitions, even when it appears to be obvious to everyone else. And some students will just go against the crowd because that is their style—they are rebellious and like to stand out—a rebel without a cause. If you notice any students displaying these behaviors, address the issue in private to determine their motivation and address it as appropriate.

PRACTICING ASSERTIVE STATEMENTS

Up to this point, the students have been taught the importance of expressing their personal thoughts and feelings assertively. They have had a chance to physically understand these concepts through hand-shaking and Hi-5s and had training in hearing the different styles of communication. Now they will practice speaking assertively.

The students will express the physical and verbal qualities of being assertive using prepared statements. Their task is to read the statements assertively, using a calm expression and appropriate qualities of body language, eye contact, and tone of voice.

 Materials:
paper or
index cards
with assertive
statements on them
(see Resource B)

GOAL: Students will assertively say prepared statements.

 Time: 15 minutes

ACTIVITY

1 Remind the students to be aware of the five qualities of assertive communication:

- Be calm
- Body language
- Eye contact
- Tone of voice
- Say what you want

2 When they make their statements, the students should be standing up straight, both feet on the floor. Later on, when they are more proficient, they can experiment with their own personal style.

Hand out one assertive statement card to each student. Give the students a minute to review the card and consider how to make the statement using the five qualities of assertiveness. When it is their turn, the student will stand up and address you. They may either make the statement from memory or read directly from the card. The words they use don't have to be exactly those written on the card, but they should be close. Watch to see if they show the qualities of assertive communication. Respectfully critique their responses, understanding that this first try out loud might be awkward. Communicating assertively takes practice and is a continual work in progress.

Lesson Extension

1. After the student reads the card, ask, *"When would you have to make a statement like this?"* The goal of this question is to make it clear that this skill is relevant in their everyday life.

2. Students like to offer the aggressive way of how the statements could be read—this can be quite fun. As time allows, let them offer examples of how they could make the statement aggressively, but be clear that swear words and violent actions are not acceptable. Ask them what it might sound or look like if they were to be passive in the situation indicated on the card. Always end by having the student say the statement assertively to reinforce the expected and appropriate style.

Assertive Statements: (NOTE: Each scenario is represented on its own square in Resource B so that teachers may photocopy and hand out individual cards.)

1. Thank you for asking, but I do not want to play right now.

2. Please do not speak to me like that.

3. Thank you, but I do not like broccoli.

4. I am very tired. I don't want to be teased right now.

5. I would rather not hang out with those people. Let's do something else.

6. I don't think it's the right thing to do and I don't want to do it.

7. I don't want to do that. But let's see if we can compromise.

8. Please do not play with my things.

9. If you are going to play with my games, please put them away when you are finished.

10. For my birthday I would like to receive a video game.

11. I want pizza for dinner. Thank you for asking.

12. Thank you for asking, but I am not interested in going to that party.

13. I'm in a bad mood today. I would like to spend the day by myself.

14. Please don't interrupt when I am talking.

15. I don't like movies like that. Let's find one that we both like.

16. I like you a lot, but I don't like when you tease me.

17. How about spaghetti tonight, and tomorrow we will have sandwiches?

18. I can't talk on the phone now. I'll see you tomorrow.

19. That's cheating, but I would be happy to help you study.

20. That embarrasses me. Please don't do that in front of other people.

21. Thank you, but I was told not to talk to strangers.

22. I have a headache; I would rather just take a nap. But thank you for asking.

23. When you don't ask my opinion, it makes me feel unimportant.

24. I really like you, but I don't like the decision you made.

25. Excuse me. I was in line first. Please don't go in front of me.

26. I need to finish this job. I will be happy to help you when I am finished.

27. That sounds great, but I've got other plans this weekend.

28. Let's all play together.

29. Can my friend join in?

30. Let's let the younger kids play.

31. Let's make room so Taylor can sit here, too.

32. Please stop making faces at me. I don't like it.

33. Can I play too?

34. Leave my backpack alone.

35. That's my spot in line.

36. Excuse me, would you please move your papers over to your part of the table?

37. Do you want to go to the movies on Saturday?

38. Do you want to go skiing with me next weekend?

39. Excuse me, where is the bathroom?

40. Maybe we can get together another time.

41. May I borrow your pencil?

42. May I pet your dog?

43. Let's not talk about other people when they're not here.

Final Thoughts

On more than one occasion, we have entered a class to teach assertiveness only to have the teacher bellow a command to the students: "SIT DOWN AND BE QUIET! THESE PEOPLE ARE TAKING TIME OUT OF THEIR BUSY DAY, AND I WON'T HAVE YOU BEING RUDE AND DISRESPECTFUL!" Yikes! The students are quite cooperative, but we know that the lesson will not be as effective as we had hoped. Remember, the best way to increase assertive communication is to discuss the expectation and role model it all the time.

Ask your friends and colleagues what they think about your style of communication, especially around students. Use these comments to evaluate your style of communication and what types of behavior you are role modeling.

ASSERTIVENESS ROLE-PLAYS

This activity teaches assertive communication through role-playing realistic scenarios. Similar to the strategy explored during the ABCD exercise, this is an opportunity for students to practice responding assertively in a nonemotional or crisis situation.

Role-playing is one of the most important aspects of developing confidence in the ability to use assertiveness skills. There is no guarantee that a person will always be assertive, especially during a challenging moment or during intense emotion, but having practiced communicating assertively will increase the odds that the person will act more assertive in their everyday life and at challenging moments.

Materials:
Scenarios cards
(see Resource C)

GOAL: Students will practice communicating assertively.

Time: 30 minutes

ACTIVITY

1 Tell the students that they will be role-playing situations that call for an assertive response. Put two chairs in front of the room. That will be the stage.

2 Explain that you, the teacher, will play the other person in the role-play, be it parent, sister, brother, friend, schoolmate, teacher, etc. The job of the student is to express their thoughts and respond to anything you might say in an assertive manner. One by one, each student will meet you on "the stage" to do their role-play.

3 Hand out the role-playing scenario cards. Give the students a few minutes to consider how they would respond if they were really in the situation. You should be familiar with all the cards and be ready to respond when the role-play begins.

4 Begin with volunteers, but ultimately everyone needs to practice with you. The role-plays might be very quick, especially if done well, or they may take a few minutes with some class discussion. This is a great interactive learning opportunity for all.

Make it clear that if a student does not want to role-play in front of others, they need to assertively let you know that they wish to pass. They may simply state, from their seats, using the qualities of assertive communication, "I pass." This demonstrates your respect for their feelings and role models mutual respect. However, you need to also tell students who opt out of the exercise that you will work on the exercise together in private, at another time. It is still a lesson that has to be learned and practiced.

Assertive Communication Scenarios

1. Someone steps in front of you in the lunch line.

2. You are hanging out with some people. A couple of them light up a cigarette and ask you if you want to smoke. You do not want to.

3. Your friend keeps making comments to you during a movie or a TV show.

4. Your parent asks you to do a chore, but your favorite show is about to start.

5. Someone taunts you about a body part, and you don't like it.

6. Your brother or sister has been using the computer for a long time and you would like to use it.

7. Your sibling is on the computer IMing about "stuff." You need the computer for a homework assignment, and it is getting late.

8. A teacher accuses you of something you did not do.

9. You believe a former friend is saying mean things about you to other people.

10. A friend invites themself to sleep over, and you would rather they didn't.

11. You are eating dinner at a friend's house, and they serve you something you really don't like.

12. You are spending the night with friends, and someone suggests you raid the parent's liquor cabinet.

13. Your teacher gives you a poor grade on an essay test. You feel it was unfair.

14. Your parent is serving the same food three nights in a row. You didn't like it the first two nights, and definitely don't want it tonight.

15. Your mom goes to give you a hug and kiss in front of all your friends, and you are embarrassed.

16. Your friend calls you a nickname you don't like.

17. You come home from school and find that your younger brother or sister played with a game of yours that was in your room and is supposed to be off-limits.

18. Your brother or sister left your magazine outside, and it got ruined when it rained.

19. A bunch of other students are saying things to another student and causing them to cry. This is really bothering you.

20. Your friends want to see a movie you know your parents would not approve of, and you want to respect your parents' wishes.

Final Thoughts

Teaching assertiveness skills without actually practicing them would be like teaching a child how to play basketball from charts and still expecting the child to perform well during a big game. If students don't practice assertive communication, we can't expect them to act respectfully and respond effectively during challenging moments in their lives. By practicing assertive communication with your students, you will make your job easier, you will enjoy your job more, the students will behave more respectfully, they will enjoy school more, and they will achieve greater academic success; a pretty good investment for the time and effort.

STATISTICS AND STUDIES

- In "... more than ... two-thirds of 37 shootings, the attackers felt 'persecuted, bullied, threatened, attacked, or injured by others,' and that revenge was an underlying motive." (Lyznicki, McCaffree, & Robinowitz, 2004)
- Children and youth who are bullied are typically anxious, insecure, and cautious and suffer from low self-esteem, rarely defending themselves or retaliating when confronted by students who bully them. (Olweus, 1993)
- Children and youth who are bullied are often socially isolated and lack social skills. (Nansel, et al., 2001)
- Bullying was reported as more prevalent among males than females and occurred with greater frequency among middle school-aged youth than high school-aged youth. For males, both physical and verbal bullying was common, while for females, verbal bullying and rumors were more common. (Nansel, et al., 2001)
- Eighty-seven percent said shootings are motivated by a desire to "get back at those who have hurt them." (Shaw, 2003)
- Eight-six percent said, "other kids picking on them, making fun of them, or bullying them" causes teenagers to turn to lethal violence in the schools. (Shaw, 2003)
- Bullying occurred most frequently in sixth through eighth grades, with little variation between urban, suburban, town, and rural areas; suburban youth were 2 to 3 percent less likely to bully others. Males were both more likely to bully others and more likely to be victims of bullying than were females. In addition, males were more likely to say they had been bullied physically (being hit, slapped, or pushed), while females more frequently said they were bullied verbally and psychologically (through sexual comments or rumors). (National Institutes of Health, 2001)

Responding to a Bully 6

Bullying happens. Regardless of policies, programs, or threat of consequences, some students will bully, or attempt to bully others. The people they choose to bully are people they believe will not or cannot stand up for themselves. Bullies commonly look for students who may be considered weird or different, or who don't fit in. These students usually lack the knowledge, confidence, or skills to assertively stand up to a bully and stop the bullying behavior. They are not good at spontaneously reacting to a bullying episode, and sometimes, when they do attempt to stand up to a bully, their style actually makes the bullying worse.

Some students get bullied for other reasons, such as being in the wrong place at the wrong time. Regardless of the reason, it will be the reaction of the targeted student that will determine if they continue to get bullied.

One reaction, often reinforced by the media and even some adults, is to stand up to the bully with "one quick punch." It is believed that by doing so the bully will gain respect for or develop fear of the target and stop the bullying. However, a violent response to bullying will often result in more violence as well as trouble with authority. A more effective strategy to reduce bullying is to empower the targets.

This section uses the qualities discussed in Chapter 5, Teaching Assertiveness, to teach students how to respond to the most common type of direct bullying—threats and verbal bullying—in a manner that minimizes a recurrence of bullying or having it escalate into a physical altercation. The plan is nonviolent and effective and teaches students to be self-reliant in dealing with challenges.

Role-playing opportunities for the students will follow the detailed explanation of the lesson. Some students may need extra role-playing opportunities, perhaps in private. This step is vital. To reduce victimization, students must be prepared, confident, and proficient in how to effectively respond to direct bullying behavior.

BULLY PROOFING PLAN OF ACTION

The Bully Proofing Plan of Action helps students limit their exposure to bullying. It is effective because it teaches students to be self-reliant and nonviolent.

You will find this lesson most effective if you work with an adult partner. This lesson is not only educational but can also be very entertaining. Prior to teaching this lesson, discuss with your partner how you want to be bullied. Your partner should be prepared to stop the bullying for each section of the lesson and know when to continue, depending on which aspect of the strategy is being discussed.

 Materials:
paper (per student)
pencil (per student)
another adult

GOAL: Students will role-play The Bully Proofing Plan of Action.

 Time: 60 minutes

ACTIVITY

1 Tell the students that they will learn how to respond to someone who is *directly* bullying them by calling them names, challenging them to a fight, making fun of them, or pressuring them to do something they do not want to do. You will also suggest the order in which you expect them to respond. However, each bullying situation is different, and therefore, the students have to determine the best and safest way to respond in each bullying situation.

2 Review the definition of bully and bullying with the students:
Bully:
- a person who hurts or frightens other, weaker people
- a cruel and brutal person
- one habitually cruel to others who are weaker

Bullying:
- behavior that ridicules, humiliates, or harms another person; may be repeated over time
- to discourage or frighten with threats
- systematically and chronically inflicting physical hurt and/or psychological distress on one or more people
- to intimidate with superior strength

Review the different *types* of bullying with the students:

Physical
- Physical bullying is action oriented. It includes hitting, kicking, spitting, pushing, or taking or damaging a person's property.

Verbal
- Verbal bullying is the use of words to hurt or humiliate another person. It includes name-calling, insulting, put-downs, and making threats or rude comments.

Relational (also known as Social Aggression)
- Relational bullying is the use of relationships to hurt others. It includes using the silent treatment, preventing people from playing with others, and spreading rumors and lies.

Cyber
- Cyber bullying is the use of technology to hurt or humiliate others. It includes using computers and the Internet, e-mails, Instant Messaging (IM), cell phones (i.e., text messaging), and digital photography to embarrass or exclude others.

③ The Severity Clause

Instruct the students to write on their paper what you write on the board.

On the board write Bully Proofing Plan of Action. Toward the bottom of the board, write Severity clause: Protect your body at all times. Leave space for other choices you will be writing (See Figure 6.1).

Figure 6.1

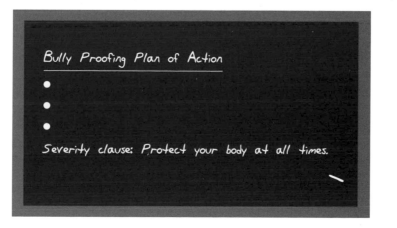

Violence does not
prevent violence;
violence begets
violence.

The severity clause means that you should protect your body at all times.

Suggested Script:

If you are being physically attacked, it is OK to use self-defense to protect your body and get yourself to safety. Protecting your body does not mean that you continue to hit or kick if you gain the physical advantage, such as if the bully falls to the ground. It also does not mean that you may use a weapon.

A lot of bullying is verbal and designed to upset a person or to get the other person to throw the first punch so the bully can claim self-defense when they hit back. Regardless of what the bully says, if you hit a person who is verbally attacking you, you will get in trouble. Responding physically to verbal bullying is not self-defense.

The following strategies are in the most common order used for responding to a bully. The strategies may be used in a different order than suggested.

Bullies want to see
their target get upset.
Do not fall into
the trap!

4 The most common type of bullying is verbal, i.e., put downs, name-calling, insults, and threats of violence. Often, the goal of the verbal bully is to manipulate the target—either by seeing the target upset, engaging the target in a verbal or physical confrontation, or getting the target to do (or not do) something. Therefore, students need to know how to respond nonviolently and effectively to verbal bullying. On the board, below Bully Proofing Plan of Action, write Ignore and/or walk away (See Figure 6.2).

Figure 6.2

> Bully Proofing Plan of Action
> • Ignore and/or walk away
> •
> •
> Severity clause: Protect your body at all times.

Many parents and school staff encourage children to ignore verbal taunts. Unfortunately, they rarely explain the details of what ignoring looks like, nor do they role-play how to ignore taunts. Due to this lack of detail and practice, the strategy often fails, and sometimes the situation is made worse.

Conversely, some people believe that ignoring verbal bullying is not acceptable. They believe that a person cannot allow another person to "dis" or disrespect them, their friends, or their family. Some people believe that if someone says something insulting or threatening, a person *has to* respond in kind—not only to maintain self-respect, but to stop the abuse.

For two reasons we suggest ignoring the taunts:

1. Students who are consistently targeted rarely have the skills to respond in kind, and their attempts are often considered lame and actually perpetuate the taunting.

2. If a student responds in kind to verbal taunting, there is a good chance that the situation will escalate with the targeted student losing.

This said, *how* a person ignores someone who is taunting them is key. Ignoring someone who is trying to verbally bully you takes a lot of self-control. How to ignore verbal bullying needs to be taught and practiced.

> Learning martial arts is an excellent bully proofing strategy. Students who learn martial arts often develop the skills, confidence, and social network that reduce the chances of being targeted.

Suggested Script:

> One way to stop verbal bullying is to ignore it. Do not show strong emotion, do not respond with mean comments or throw the first punch. The bully wants you to take those actions, so don't do it! If a bully sees you turn red, cry, respond with your own put-downs or threats, or become violent, the bully will have succeeded and will continue to bully you. You haven't stopped the bullying, you have reinforced it.
>
> Ignoring a bully is active, not passive. It is not wimping out. The bully is trying to use words to trap you. By ignoring the bully, you choose not to fall for the trap. If the bullying stops, you have solved your problem. It is a victory for you. Feel proud.

> Ignoring verbal taunts can limit its continuation, but it may still cause anguish. Awareness and management of emotions associated with taunting should be discussed with the students.

How to Ignore an Aggressor

Explain and demonstrate the do's and don'ts of the strategy to your students.

The Details of Ignoring

Suggested Script:

WHAT TO DO:

> If someone begins to say mean things to you, continue to do whatever it was that you were doing before the bullying began. This is a good strategy if the bully is making comments when walking by.

swinging high and an exaggerated stride. This should get a laugh from the class and that is the point. Not only did you entertain the bully, but the bystanders too. This type of reaction encourages the bully to bully again.

Demonstrate the correct way to walk away:
Begin the scenario again. The bully will come up to you and stand beside you saying insults. After five seconds of ignoring the bully, turn and walk away. Walk toward the imaginary adults with your head up, your back straight, and at a normal walking pace.

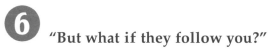 **"But what if they follow you?"**

How to Assertively Say, "Stop!" and Walk Away

On the board, write, "Assertively say 'Stop!' *and* walk away." (See Figure 6.3).

Figure 6.3

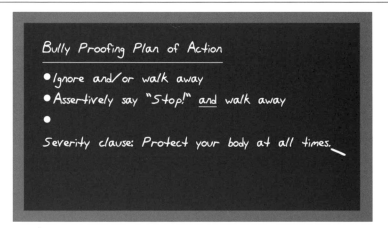

Suggested Script:

When you choose to walk away from the person who is trying to bully you, expect that the person will continue to say mean things. Continue to ignore the comments and walk toward people you believe will provide safety. As you are walking, listen and look through the corner of your eye to decide if the bully is following you. If the bully follows you for more than ten or fifteen steps, be prepared to speak up. As you are walking, think about how you will tell the bully to stop. Decide where you will stop to turn toward the bully, how you will position yourself, and what you will say.

Also, there are times when you cannot or should not ignore or walk away from the bully. There are times when the first thing you should do is tell the bully to stop. For instance, if you have waited twenty minutes for your turn to use a computer, and a bully hassles you to use the computer, you should not have to walk away. Or if a bully is wadding up paper and throwing it at you, ignoring or walking away without saying anything may be considered weak. Situations like these call for assertive communication. When you tell the bully to stop, say it assertively and position yourself in a way that protects your body if the bully physically attacks you.

Say and demonstrate the following:
When you are ready to tell the bully to stop, turn toward the bully and stop turning when you are at a 45° angle—do not directly face the bully. Also, maintain a distance of 1½ to 2 arm lengths. The reasons for this positioning are as follows:

1. *Standing at a 45° angle protects your body if the bully continues to walk toward you. If the bully does continue to move toward you, you can side-step, while still retaining balance, and maintain a safe distance of 1½ to 2 arm lengths from the bully. It is a disadvantage to face the bully directly because to maintain a safe distance, you would have to step back. Stepping back might put you off balance, and you could trip or fall into something.*

2. *Standing at a 45° angle to the bully provides some protection for your body in case the bully decides to become physically violent. If you are directly facing the bully, and the bully throws a punch or tries to kick you, your eyes, nose, throat, chest, stomach, and private areas are easy targets for the bully. If you are standing at a 45° angle, there is a better chance that the arm or the side of the body will get hit, not the more vulnerable areas. This is a common self-defense technique.*

3. *Maintaining a distance of 1½ to 2 arm lengths gives you some room to block or deflect contact if the bully tries to hit or grab you.*

Once you have turned toward the bully, say, "Stop!" or, "Leave me alone!" or, "Cut it out!" This must be said using strong body language, eye contact, and tone of voice.

Be Calm: *In a bullying situation, you might be nervous or become quite angry; still, you have to appear calm and in control. It will be easier to be calm and have confidence if you role-play being bullied while practicing the qualities of assertiveness. Also, remind yourself that the bully is setting a trap for you and wants you to become upset, so you have to work hard to remain calm. A quiet, deep breath might help you to remain calm.*

Body Language: *Use body language that communicates strength and seriousness—head up, back straight, arms down in front or beside you, and feet at shoulder width. By having arms in front or beside you, they are available if needed for protection. Feet at shoulder width will help you maintain balance.*

DO NOT:

- *Lean toward the person in a threatening way*
- *Shift your weight back and forth on your legs or hips—like a strange dance or like you really need to go to the bathroom, a.k.a. The Pee Dance*
- *Fold your arms across your chest*
- *Rest your hands on your hips*
- *Move your hands or head around*
- *Have your hands in your pockets*
- *Point at the bully*
- *Stand as if you are a soldier at attention or stiff as a statue*

Figure 6.4

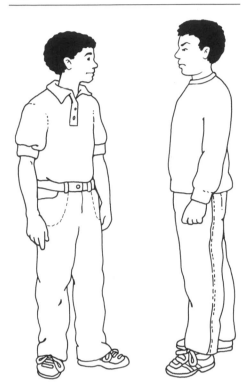

Eye Contact: *Look the person in the eye. Eye contact shows confidence and strength, something most bullies do not expect. This is important even if you are nervous. Maintain eye contact as you tell the bully, "Stop," or, "Cut it out!" which should only take about one or two seconds. If looking in the eye of the bully is too difficult, make eye contact with an area very close to the eyes, such as eyebrows or nose.*

DO NOT:

- *Stare, glare, attempt to intimidate, or make the other person uncomfortable with too much eye contact—three to four seconds at one time would be considered too long*
- *Look at the ceiling or something in the distance*
- *Look at your shoes or the floor*
- *Move your eyes too much*
- *Roll your eyes*

Tone of Voice: *Use a steady tone and speak clearly. Speak loudly enough for the bully to hear you. You can also choose to speak loudly enough, without yelling, to get the attention of a nearby adult.*

DO NOT:

- *Yell or scream*
- *Talk too softly*
- *Speak too fast*
- *Mumble or whine*

Say What You Want: Make short statements that are to the point, such as, "Stop!" or, "Cut it out!" or, "Leave me alone."

DO NOT:
- *Explain the consequences of bullying*
- *Quote passages from the bullying policy*
- *Insult or threaten the bully*
- *Say something sarcastic or opposite of what you really mean such as, "Yeah, keep calling me names. I really enjoy that."*

When you turn toward the bully, use strong body language, eye contact, tone of voice, and say, for example, "Stop it!" or, "Cut it out!" Then turn away from the bully and, if possible, walk away. If you walk away, walk toward a place of safety. The bully may still follow, so continue to use your eyes and ears!

It is important to emphasize the importance of all five qualities of assertive communication. If a student uses good body language and eye contact, and says the right words but speaks in a panicky, screechy, or whiny voice, it might entice the bully to continue.

Demonstrate With Your Partner

Tell the students that in your demonstration you will speed up time and work within the confines of the space available, which would be different if you were in the hall or other location.

Demonstrate the wrong way to tell a bully to stop:
Wrong way #1:
As before, stand in front of the class reading. This time the bully will come up and stand beside you saying insults. After four to six seconds of trying to ignore the bully, turn and walk away. The bully should follow and continue insulting you. Instead of turning to the bully and saying, "Stop," just keep walking away—around the room, with the bully following you.

Explain that you should not keep walking, and walking, and walking if you are continually bullied. That becomes the bully's game, and you lose.

Wrong way #2:
Begin the scenario again. Try to ignore and walk away. Have the bully follow and continue insulting you. Then turn toward the bully and say, in a panicked, screechy voice, looking at anything except the bully, *"Will you stop it already!?! You're so annoying!!"* Finally, turn and walk away with an exaggerated stride. If you do this well, you will get a laugh from your students, and you will know that you made your point.

Demonstrate the correct way to tell a bully to stop:
Begin the scenario again. After four to six seconds of trying to ignore the bully, turn and walk away. The bully will follow you. Take ten steps, or as room allows, and then turn on your 45° angle toward the bully and assertively say, "Cut it out." Then turn and walk away again, toward the imaginary adults. The bully should not follow.

Your students should know that sometimes a person has to run away.

During college, I was out with some friends. I was in a great mood, and we were all laughing about lots of things. I made a comment to a friend about her height that I meant only as a friendly tease. I restated the comment a little while later, and this time she said, assertively, "Steve, now I'm getting insulted." I realized that no one thought it was funny at all. In hindsight, I realized that she ignored the comment the first time it was said, hoping I would not repeat the comment. It wasn't until she assertively told me how she felt that I realized I had offended her. This is a perfect example of how the skills discussed in this chapter can be used in a variety of situations. I never repeated the comment, and we are still great friends. —SB

Suggested Script:

Sometimes the best defense is to just not be there. Sometimes you may have to run away. If you do decide to run, run to a trusted adult and clearly explain the situation.

7 **"But what if the bully continues to follow you?"** On the board, write, "Go to a trusted adult" (See Figure 6.4).

Figure 6.5

After explaining to students about assertively telling the bully to stop, two common questions arise: "What if they still follow you?" and, "What if the bully stops bullying you at that moment, but bullies you again later or the next day?" In other words, how often should a student tell the bully to stop before realizing it has no effect and they need another plan?

At about fourth or fifth grade, students feel that going to an adult for any challenging peer situation is seen as babyish. Some people believe that no matter what, you do not go to an adult for help with a bully. It is very important to understand this perspective, but educators don't have to accept it. Students need a nonviolent and effective option when they can't stop bullying or are facing serious danger. Adults have to discuss with students the option of working with an adult to solve their problems. For their part, adults have to instill confidence that they are a helpful resource.

Suggested Script:

Sometimes a bully will find a new way to bully—that is, the bully will force you to continually move from wherever you are to another location. They will play the game of having you tell them to stop and they will stop . . . for the moment . . . as they watch you walk away . . . again and again. The bully may not follow you when you are walking near an adult, but they may continue to bully when adults are not close by.

At this point, you have two choices. You can turn toward the bully and assertively say, "I asked you to stop. If you don't stop, I will talk to an adult," and then walk away. If the bully stops, there will be no need to talk to an adult. However, if the bullying continues, you have to tell a trusted adult. Otherwise it will be obvious that you are bluffing, and then the bully will know how to control you.

All students and adults need to know the difference between tattling and telling. See the section "Tattling vs. Telling" (page 117) to help students determine the difference.

The language suggested specifically avoids using the word "tell" as in, "I will tell an adult." The word "tell" lends itself to being considered a tattletale phrase and could easily give the bully new verbal ammunition. Using the word "talk" as in, "I will talk to an adult," is intended to limit that possibility as well as address the target's self image.

Suggested Script:

Another choice is to go to a trusted adult without warning the bully first. When speaking with an adult:

- *Remain calm*
- *Explain the situation*
- *State what steps were already tried to resolve the situation*
- *Make suggestions on how the adult can help solve the problem*

As an example, go to an adult you are comfortable with and say, "I am trying to stay out of a fight. Alex has been bothering me. I've tried ignoring, and then I walked away. Alex kept bothering me and didn't stop even when I said, "Stop," and walked away again. Like I said, I am trying to stay out of a fight. Would you talk to Alex?"

Tell your students that even adults need to talk to adults. Adults go to doctors, mechanics, therapists, lawyers and the police when they need assistance with their challenges.

Activity: Ask the children to think of adults they trust to go to with a bullying problem. Then have each student write down the names of three trusted adults, in and out of school, they can talk to about a bullying problem.

Demonstrate With Your Partner

Before beginning the demonstration, pick a student who is sitting near the back of the room to be an imaginary adult. This is the person you will go to when you have to talk to an adult about the bullying. Again, remind the students that you will be speeding up the scenario.

Demonstrate the wrong way to talk to an adult:

Begin the scenario again. When you walk away from the bully, walk directly to the "adult." When you talk to the adult, whine, snivel, and rant about how mean the bully has been and how they should be thrown out of school for being mean. For instance, in a rant and rave, say, "*Alex keeps making fun of me and calling me names. People aren't supposed to do that and I don't like it. People like that shouldn't be in school. I think Alex should be suspended right now.*" If you do this dramatically it will be obvious to the students that this is an ineffective way to describe a situation and speak to an adult.

Tell the students that if they go to an adult with a problem, and the adult does not help them resolve the problem, they need to talk to another adult.

Demonstrate the correct way to talk to an adult:

Begin the scenario again. This time the bully will come up and stand beside you stating insults. After about two to three seconds of ignoring the bully, turn and walk away. The bully will follow you. Take a few moments and then turn on your 45° angle and assertively say, "*Cut it out.*" Then turn and walk away again. This time the bully will continue to follow you. Walk toward the adult. The bully should stop following you when you get within ten to fifteen feet of the adult and walk away. Say to the adult, "*I'm trying to stay out of a fight. Alex has been bothering me. I've tried ignoring, and then I walked away. Alex kept bothering me even when I said stop. Like I said, I'm trying to stay out of a fight.*"

! Adults should not respond in a manner that will embarrass or humiliate the target or the bully. Our experience has been that when students choose not to go to adults—parents or teachers—for help in a bullying situation, it is because they fear that adults' actions will be embarrassing to the student and make the situation worse. A target wants the bullying to stop but not at the risk of social humiliation.

ROLE-PLAYING THE BULLY PROOFING PLAN OF ACTION

1 Ask for a student volunteer to role-play a bullying situation with you. You will play the bully, and the student will be the target. Tell everyone you will be acting like a bully only for the sake of teaching. Do not bully the student about any issue they are sensitive about.

Use examples below as a theme for a bullying situation. Before role-playing, consider some of the lines that you will use so that you don't have to make them all up at the moment of the role-play.

For the first role-play, pick one of the following scenarios. Play it out and stop after the target ignores, walks away, or says, "Stop," or, "Leave me alone," or, "Cut it out."

Bully the student about:
- Having a boy/girl friend
- Wearing off-brand sneakers
- Having old-style glasses
- Wearing nice jewelry and demanding they give it to you
- Doing well on a test
- Being a nerd
- Being friends with a nerd
- Being the teacher's pet

You can also bully the student by:
- Making believe the target is on the lunch line and pushing in front of them—discuss how the response by the target might differ if it was just one day or every day
- Continually doing something very annoying, such as making threatening faces, kicking their shoes, or making believe you are touching the target's hair
- Trying to get the target to smoke or drink alcohol

Remind the student volunteer of the Bully Proofing Plan of Action. If they forget what to do, they can look at the board where the choices are still written.

Do these demonstrations with a few different students using different bullying situations and styles. Vary the timing of when you back off from the target and how long you continue to bully.

Also, begin some scenarios with immediate bullying and others scenarios by starting out friendly, creating a false sense of security for the target, and then act like a bully. For instance, "Hey, Asa. How are you doing? You look good today. I need money. Give me some money. Don't be a cheapskate. I know you have some. Come on, give me some. Don't act so stuck-up."

2 After a few role-plays with you, have the students practice the Bully Proofing Plan of Action with each other. Explain the following instructions while the students are still in their seats. After the instructions are explained, pair up the students and lead them through each step.

1. The two students in each pair determine whose name comes first in the alphabet. The person whose name comes first will be Student "A," the other person is Student "B."

Using the terms "mean name," "put-down," and "insult" during the role-plays will avoid misunderstandings between the students.

2. To begin, Student "A" will be the bully; Student "B" will be the target.

3. **First role-play:** The bully will say to the target, "Mean name, mean name," and the target will turn and walk four to five steps with their head up, back straight and a normal walking pace. The bully will just stay put. After practicing this step, the target will return and prepare the second part of the role-play.

4. **Second role-play:** Again, the bully will say to the target, "Mean name, mean name," and the target will turn and walk away. But this time the bully will follow the target, repeating, "Mean name," even more tauntingly. After three to four steps, depending on available space, the target will turn toward the bully and say, "Stop it," or something similar; this is a good opportunity for the students to find the words they are most comfortable using. Then the target will turn and walk another two steps away from the bully. The bully *will not follow.*

5. **Have the students reverse roles.** Now, Student "A" will be the target and Student "B" will be the bully.

6. **Third and fourth role-plays:** The scenes will play out exactly like before, with the students playing the opposite role. This time, have the bully say, "Put down, put down," or, "Insult, insult," instead of, "Mean name, mean name."

Final Thoughts

In a real bullying situation, powerful emotions such as anger, fear, and anxiety may surface. Talk to the students about the importance of acknowledging and expressing these feelings in a healthy manner. Review ideas discussed in Chapter 4, Emotional Control and Anger Management, which can help alleviate the strong emotions associated with a bullying experience.

A Note About Other Strategies

Some authors suggest agreeing with the bully's taunts to diffuse the situation. We don't like people to agree with a verbal put-down because it means that the target begins to self-bully. This might be a useful strategy if the target already has good self-esteem and the bullying is more of a rare occurrence. For students who have self-esteem issues, this type of response could be self-defeating.

Humor can also be a good defense against bullying. Those people who are good at being funny or can quickly come up with a witty comment or funny observation are not usually bullied for long. However, it is very difficult to teach someone to be funny or make others laugh. Therefore, we talk about it as a possibility, but it is not something we teach.

STATISTICS AND STUDIES

- Forty percent of bullied students in elementary and 60 percent of bullied students in middle school report that teachers intervene in bullying incidents "once in a while" or "almost never." (Olweus, 1993; Charach, Pepler, & Ziegler, 1995)
- Sixty-six percent of youth are teased at least once a month, and nearly one-third of youth are bullied at least once a month. (Grunbaum, et al., 2002)
- Almost 25 percent of the more than 2,300 girls surveyed felt they did not know three adults they could go to for support if they were being bullied. (Girl Scout Research Institute, 2003)
- Bullying is increasingly viewed as an important contributor to youth violence, including homicide and suicide. Case studies of the shooting at Colombine High School and other U.S. schools have suggested that bullying was a factor in many of the incidents. (Bullying Statistics, n.d.)
- Surveys show that 77 percent of students are bullied mentally, verbally, and physically. (Bullying Statistics, n.d.)

Unit Test
Chapters 4, 5, 6

Circle all the ideas that are healthy ways to calm down:
- biting your lip until it bleeds
- taking deep breaths
- thinking about being in a peaceful place
- going for a walk
- writing your thoughts and feelings in a journal
- talking to an adult you trust
- punching a wall
- exercising
- yelling at someone smaller than you

Put a checkmark next to the correct answers. Slow, deep breathing is good for:
____ staying calm
____ getting angrier
____ helping to think about how to solve a problem
____ helping to reduce stress
____ annoying others around you

There are five qualities to assertiveness. Put a check mark next to each.
____ making eye contact
____ being smart
____ being calm and in control
____ using a neutral tone of voice
____ being very tall
____ saying what you want
____ having money
____ having big muscles
____ waving your arms
____ being cute
____ yelling
____ using strong body language

Why is communicating assertively useful?

_____

_____

_____

_____

Put a checkmark next to the correct answers:

_____ Assertive communication is a respectful way to tell people what you are thinking or feeling.

_____ Saying, "Like it or not, we are playing this game and this game only!" is an assertive statement.

_____ Saying, "OK, I guess you can borrow my books," even though you do not want to lend them out is acting assertively.

_____ Calmly saying, "Please stop that. It really bothers me," is an assertive statement.

List two examples of aggressive communication.

_____

_____

_____

_____

List two examples of passive communication.

_____

_____

_____

_____

List the three steps of the Bully Proofing Plan of Action.

_____

_____

_____

_____

**Severity clause: Protect your body at all times.
Explain the meaning of the severity clause.

_____

_____

_____

_____

The Power of 7
Bystanders

He who passively accepts evil is as much involved in it as he who helps to perpetrate it.

—MARTIN LUTHER KING, JR.

A bystander is a person who is present at an event without participating in it. Even though they are not participants, bystanders have a tremendous amount of power and influence, especially in regard to bullying. Along with the response of the target, it is the action or inaction of bystanders that will determine if bullying continues or ends.

Research shows that most students do nothing about bullying they witness or know about unless there is serious danger. Some of the reasons bystanders do not respond to bullying is because they:

- don't know what to do, what to say, or who to tell;
- are not sure if they should involve adults;
- are afraid if they get involved they will also become a target of bullying;
- are afraid involvement might make the situation worse for the target;
- may consider the bully a friend;
- are not friends with the target;
- don't consider bullying, or a particular bullying episode, to be a problem for themselves;
- consider the target a loser, nerd, geek, etc.;
- do not believe the target deserves empathy;
- think the target "asks" for it through their actions (provocative victim);
- think the bullying will toughen the target up;
- think targets need to learn how to stand up for themselves;
- believe that kids don't tell on other kids;
- feel it's a lot easier to just ignore the bullying; or

- weren't asked for help and are not volunteering help.

A culture of noninvolvement produces an acceptance of wrongdoing that perpetuates wrongdoing.

Students concerned about social status, self-protection, and maintaining any spoken or unspoken community or "kid" culture believe these are good reasons to remain uninvolved. School personnel who show they understand this concern are respected by their students. In turn, this offers an opportunity to present *another* viewpoint: the values and expectations of the school community that include helping another person who is suffering and maintaining a safe school for everyone. Teaching the expectation of helping targets of bullying reinforces the value of empathy.

The lessons in this chapter, along with appropriate responses by adults when asked to be involved, reinforces a culture where bullying and other hurtful behavior is "everybody's business" and will not be tolerated. In turn, this positively impacts academic success, feelings of physical and emotional safety, and responsible citizenship.

The steps outlined in this chapter are designed to empower bystanders to help a target of bullying while minimizing risk to all involved. However, sometimes the risk is greater than anticipated. Throughout the lesson, remind students to consider these risks before determining which action to take. At no time are you expecting them to do anything violent or put themselves in jeopardy.

WHAT'S A BYSTANDER TO DO?

In this lesson the students will learn how to respond if they are bystanders of bullying. You will demonstrate how to effectively intervene, offering specific language and physical actions that will help stop a bullying situation, maintain a high degree of physical and emotional safety, and build self-esteem. The students will also learn the difference between tattling and telling and how to determine when telling an adult about the actions of another is warranted.

Research shows that 95 percent of students witness verbal bullying, 68 percent witness physical bullying, and 48 percent of secondary school students report witnessing physical sexual coercion.

Materials per student:
paper
pencil

> **GOAL: Students will be able to articulate the five expected responses if they are bystanders of bullying.**

Time: 45 minutes

ACTIVITY

1 Suggested Script:

Most students are not bullies, and most students do not get bullied on a regular basis. But bullying does happen, and usually other students know about it. Most bullies prefer to have others around to impress, receive encouragement or acceptance from, or to join in on the bullying. The people who see or are aware of bullying are called bystanders.

Bystanders have a lot of power; enough power to help end bullying without putting themselves at great risk. With a few simple strategies, bystanders can be the school's most powerful tool in stopping bullying.

At this school, all students are expected to try to prevent or stop bullying. We will discuss various ways you can help stop bullying in a safe and effective way.

Research shows that when a bystander tells a bully to stop the bullying, it reduces bullying about 75 percent.

Review the types of bullying, as necessary. See Chapter 1, "Same Page" Understanding of Violence, Respect, and Bullying, for a definition and examples of bullying.

2 Instruct the students to write what you write on the board. On the board write: "What's A Bystander to Do?"

Below that, write: "Don't join in—remove yourself." (See Figure 7.1)

Figure 7.1

Suggested Script:

At the very least, if you witness bullying, do not join in. If you do nothing to help the target, do not make the situation worse. It is important to know that in most schools if you encourage the bully, you are also considered to be bullying. If you stand around and watch while someone else is bullying, it is considered giving the bully permission to continue bullying. In this class, if you stand around and laugh at someone being bullied, or even if you don't say a word, you are part of the problem.

If you do not do anything to stop the bullying, walk away from the situation. If the bullying is social aggression in the form of gossip, remove yourself from the conversation. If someone sends you mean Instant Messages (IM) about someone else, change the subject or end the conversation by signing off. If someone tells you to do something rude to someone else, don't do it.

To ignore bullying is to condone bullying.

We want students to take an action that directly prevents or stops bullying, but we offer the students this "out" so that we can show an understanding of the challenges bystanders face. By offering this option we hope to create greater buy-in and ultimately encourage more student involvement. However, as stated to the students, removing oneself from a bullying situation is better than standing by, watching, and therefore condoning bullying behavior.

Be aware of your tone of voice when describing your expectations. The goal of this lesson is to encourage students to take responsible and helpful action. Students can become defensive or feel guilty about actions they have or haven't taken in the past in regard to bullying. Be sensitive to their feelings and forgiving about past actions—or lack thereof—yet clearly state future expectations.

3 To the list on the board, add: "Tell the bullying person to 'Stop.'" (See Figure 7.2)

Figure 7.2

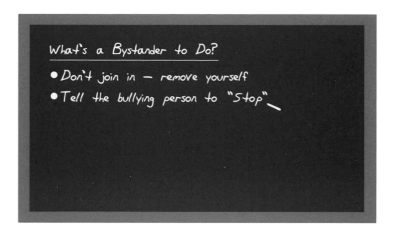

Suggested Script:

Here are other things you can do if someone is being bullied and you feel confident you can help them safely. Safely means that you will not put yourself at risk of getting bullied or hurt. It also means you will not use physical or verbal violence in the attempt to stop the bullying.

One way to stop someone from being bullied is to tell the bully to stop bullying. You might say, "C'mon, leave them alone," or, "That's not cool," or, "We don't do that here." Notice that the sentences are short and to the point. They are not lectures or preachy; they simply tell the bully to stop. Also, don't use the word "bully," as in, "Stop bullying them," or, "We don't bully others here." Sometimes people get bothered by the use of that word, and it could make the situation worse.

The level of difficulty or risk in standing up to a bully may depend on your relationship to the bully. It will be fairly easy if you are friendly with the bully, have influence over the bully, and are not worried about affecting your place in the group. On the other hand, if you are a stranger to the bully or don't believe you have any special influence, telling the bully to stop might be difficult and could put you at risk of being bullied. Even so, if you don't know the bully but feel confident that you will not put yourself at risk, telling a bully to "Stop," in an assertive, nonthreatening manner can be a very effective way to stop bullying.

Demonstrate:

Ask a student volunteer to stand right next to another student volunteer who is sitting down. Have the standing student look down in a menacing style at the sitting student (only use students who you know are comfortable with each other). Bullying happens when there is a difference in power and in this example the standing student represents

Some countries require citizens to assist people in distress, or call an emergency number, unless doing so would put them in harm's way.

greater power by looming over the sitting student and by having a look of intimidation.

You, the teacher, will play the bystander. Walk over to the bully and say something like, "*Hey, c'mon leave them alone,*" or, "*That's not cool. We don't do that here.*" Use whatever words or expressions are acceptable and realistic to your students. Discuss and demonstrate that sometimes even just a look—eye contact—and a back and forth shake of the head can communicate, "Stop."

Tell the students to expect that even if the bullying ends, the bully might feel a need to get in the last word such as, "Yeah, I'm just wasting my time with this loser, anyway." As we discussed during the Bully Proofing Plan of Action lesson in Chapter 6, the target and now the bystander too should just ignore the comment.

At this point, expect "What if" questions from the students. Ask them to hold off asking questions until later in the lesson. Many of their questions will be answered as you continue the lesson.

4 Add to the list on the board: "Separate the bullying student away from the person being bullied." (See Figure 7.3)

Figure 7.3

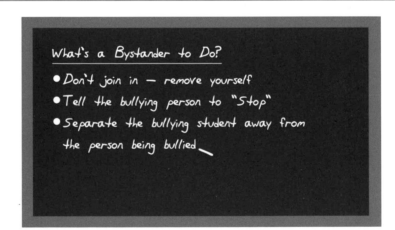

Suggested Script:

> *Another choice is to separate the bully from the person being bullied.*
> *This is a variation on telling the bully to "Stop." It is redirecting the attention of the bully away from the target by saying something like, "Hey, c'mon, let's go play tetherball," or, "Let's go see what's going on over there." This is most effective if the bystander and the bully are familiar with each other and the redirection would be considered realistic.*
> *Once again, expect that the bully might feel a need to get in the last word or insult. As mentioned earlier, the target and the bystander should ignore the comment.*

Demonstrate:

Once again, using student volunteers to represent a standing bully and a sitting target, walk up to the bully and say, *"C'mon. Let's go play basketball,"* or *"Let's go see what Jamie is up to."* If appropriate, put your hand on the bully's shoulder and guide the bully away. The bystander and the bully should take a few steps away from the target.

Point out that the redirection is stated quickly, and you should both walk away quickly. Sometimes it may take a little longer to redirect the bully; a little persistence and a few extra seconds might be all that is needed to remove the bully.

Many students are friends with a person who sometimes bullies. It is possible to like someone, but not like when they bully.

5 Add to the list on the board: "Separate the person being bullied away from the bully(s)." (See Figure 7.4)

Figure 7.4

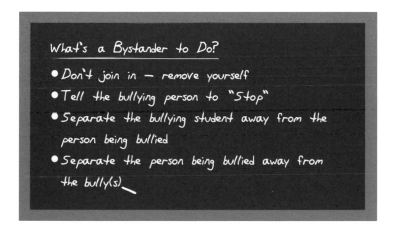

What's a Bystander to Do?

- Don't join in — remove yourself
- Tell the bullying person to "Stop"
- Separate the bullying student away from the person being bullied
- Separate the person being bullied away from the bully(s)

Suggested Script:

This step is a variation on the previous choice. Instead of redirecting or trying to stop the bully, this choice focuses on getting the target out of harm's way.

The bystander should walk up to the target and say something like, "C'mon. Let's get out of here," and walk the target away. Walk with your head up, back and shoulders straight, and focused on going to another location. If you speak or look at the bully, don't be aggressive. Remember, you are trying to stop a problem, not create a new one. Expect to hear some comments from the bully as you walk away such as, "Does baby need a protector?" or, "Can't fight your own battles?" Again, it is best to ignore these comments, but be aware of being followed. If you are followed, use the Bully Proofing Plan of Action.

There are some risks to this choice. Removing the target should be used only if you have confidence that this action, or your influence or social status, will prevent ongoing bullying.

Demonstrate:

Again, walk up to the standing bully and sitting target. Using the qualities of assertiveness, face the target and say, *"C'mon, let's get out of here."* The target should stand up and together you should walk away with head up, back and shoulders straight, focused on going to another location. As you walk, mention that you are aware of being followed. Say to the students that if you were being followed, you would use The Bully Proofing Plan of Action.

Variation: As a bystander, you could say to the target, *"Maybe you should just leave. This is not a good place for you to be right now."* Sometimes targets get nervous, freeze, and need this reminder. With this strategy, you are still helping to remove the target but you do not have to remove yourself.

6 To the list on the board, add: "Report to a trusted adult." (See Figure 7.5)

Figure 7.5

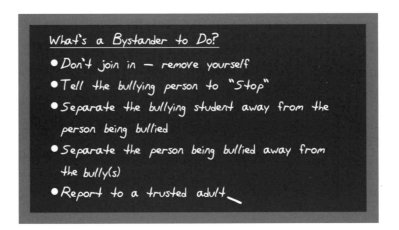

Suggested Script:

There are times when you will witness bullying or know about a particular bullying situation, and you will not feel it is safe to get directly involved. That is understandable.

If you see or know about bullying, but do not want to directly confront the bully or the target, I expect that you will go to an adult you trust and tell them the situation. You can do this in a variety of ways. For instance:

- *You can report the names of the people involved, the place where the bullying is happening, and the type of bullying. For instance, "Pat is threatening Chris in the bathroom." You are giving names, place, and the type of bullying. This is specific and detailed information.*

- *Tell an adult where bullying is taking place. For instance, "Teacher, you should check out what's going on in the bathroom." You did not give*

Teach your students to start their sentence with, "This is an emergency," if they believe an immediate response is absolutely necessary.

names, but you told an adult where they need to go to stop bullying that is happening right now.

- *You can write a note to a trusted adult about the bullying. Either write your name or leave your name off the note. This is acceptable if there is no immediate bullying situation going on, but more of an ongoing situation such as gossip, cyberbullying, stealing, exclusion, or damaging of property. Details and evidence are very helpful.*
- *Print out e-mails or IMs that are examples of someone's bullying and show them to, or leave them anonymously for, a trusted adult.*

Demonstrate:

If there is no other adult available in the classroom to assist with the demonstration, have a student volunteer be the adult. Again, you will play the bystander. Walk up to the volunteer and assertively state, *"Pat is bothering Chris in the bathroom."* Other examples are, *"You might want to check out what's going on in the hallway,"* or, *"I think you should know that Pat won't let Chris play soccer with us,"* or, *"Pat is sending e-mails to everyone that Chris wets the bed every night."*

TATTLING VS. TELLING, A.K.A. RATTING VS. REPORTING

7 **"But isn't it tattling if you tell an adult about what another student is doing?"**

This section about tattling and telling takes our lesson on a very important detour. Students need to know that there are situations when a person, child or adult, is expected to involve a person of greater authority.

Suggested Script:

> *Tattling is when a person tells about the actions of another for the purpose of getting that person in trouble. It is tattling if no one and nothing is in danger or will be in danger.*
>
> *Telling is when a person tells a person in authority that someone or something is getting hurt, or might get hurt, either physically or emotionally. A person who is telling is trying to help a person or a thing.*

A person who bullies or destroys property may say or do anything to prevent a bystander from telling. Address this point with your students and remind them not to put themselves in harm's way. Also remind them how to report bullying and other misbehavior in a subtle or anonymous manner.

Have a class discussion about which adults in the school your students consider safe people to whom they may report bullying. Invite some of these adults to class so all students can become familiar with them. Have the adults discuss how they can be informed and how they would react to being told about the actions of another student. This familiarity and assurance that some adults can help—not embarrass, humiliate, or make the situation worse—goes a long way in creating confidence that talking to a trusted adult will make the school a better place for everyone.

"Tattling," "Telling," "Ratting," or "Reporting" may not be words common to your school or student culture. Use whatever words will help differentiate the two concepts.

Suggested Script:

To make the difference between tattling and telling clear, let's use a made-up situation:

Amari and Devon are two students sitting in the back of the room. The teacher asks all the students to read pages 15–20 in their English book. Devon notices Amari is pretending to read the English book, but is actually reading a comic book. Devon goes up to the teacher and says, "Oh, Teacher, Amari is not reading what we are supposed to be reading. Amari is reading a comic book and that's not allowed during class. I just thought you should know."

This is tattling because although Amari was not following directions and breaking the class rules, Amari wasn't hurting anyone. Devon was not helping anyone avoid danger and told the teacher for the purpose of getting Amari in trouble. Although a person could argue that Devon was concerned about Amari's overall welfare and educational impact, that would be a far-fetched and unacceptable reason to tattle on Amari.

But if we take the same situation and change some of the details, it becomes telling and the correct thing to do.

Amari and Devon are two students sitting in the back of the room. The teacher asks the students to read pages 15–20 in their English book. Devon notices that Amari is quietly ripping out the wires of a nearby computer. Devon is not comfortable telling Amari to stop destroying the computer, so Devon goes up to the teacher and says, "Teacher, I think you should check out the computer in the back of the room. By the way, may I go to the bathroom?"

In this scenario, it is clear that the computer was getting damaged— property that belongs to the school. Devon did not feel safe saying anything directly to Amari to stop Amari from destroying the computer and so Devon told the teacher. In this case, Devon also asked to go to the bathroom in an attempt to make it look like that is the reason for going to the teacher. Devon is aware that telling the teacher was the responsible thing to do, but knows that Amari would be angry and may want revenge. By telling the teacher about Amari's actions and finding a reason to leave the classroom, Devon found a respectable balance between being responsible and hopefully avoiding Amari's anger.

People don't get others in trouble. A person gets in trouble due to their own actions.

"Telling" is a very challenging situation. By suggesting students ask for permission to leave the room we are offering them a safe way to take a responsible action. When students request safety by removing themselves from the situation after telling, the teacher should allow the student to leave the room. The teacher should then wait a minute before addressing the misbehaving student—unless an immediate action is necessary—in an effort to distance the teller's conversation with the teacher from the teacher's conversation with the misbehaving student.

If a student is uncomfortable saying anything to a teacher at a particular moment, even with the appearance of going elsewhere, suggest they tell the teacher later or leave a note.

Suggested Script:

> *Here's a situation to show that adults have the same bystander expectations as students.*
>
> *If I was driving and I saw someone breaking the window of a car with a big metal pipe, and taking money or property, I would call the police. Since I know the other person has a weapon—a big metal pipe—I would not want to be directly involved, so I would drive a safe distance and then make the phone call. To me, calling the police is a no-brainer. I have witnessed criminal behavior, and I have responsibility as a community member to alert the police. Besides, if I don't call the police and the thief is not caught, it might be my car that is broken into next time. I would do the same thing if I saw someone being mugged. No way would I worry about some criminal calling me a tattle-tale or a snitch. And yes, it IS my business!*
>
> *If any one of you are walking by my house and see someone climbing out of my basement window (not the person breaking into the car because I called the police and that person is already in jail) with my computer, please call the police. Please don't ignore the situation because you are afraid of being called a tattle-tale; especially since that's not tattling. That is telling or reporting, as in reporting a crime.*

Make it clear that responsible people take action when they see others hurting someone or committing a crime. These people are considered heroes. Encourage heroism.

What Is a Hero?
A hero is a person of courage or ability, admired for brave deeds or noble qualities. We honor and respect heroes because they helped another person or group of people.

Ask your students to be heroes. If someone or something is going to be hurt, ask them to take action.

Activity: What's a Bystander To Do?

8 Create groups of three or four students. Use this opportunity to have the students move to a different part of the room and work with students with whom they do not usually sit near or interact. One of the benefits of this activity is the use of positive peer pressure. If you have students who are known as cool, responsible, and mature peer leaders (high status individuals), spread them out among the groups. Some of these responsible and mature students, who are known for making good decisions, don't necessarily discuss the criteria they use to make these good decisions. This group activity is an opportunity to have others learn from these students.

On the board, write out one scenario at a time for each group to discuss. You may also pass each scenario out on a piece of paper.

By the end of the discussion of each scenario, make it clear what specific actions *you* would expect a student to take.

 Suggested Script:

Each group will discuss how students should respond if faced with this situation in real life. You can choose one of the choices previously discussed or come up with another solution that is nonviolent and effective in stopping a bully or bullying situation. During the group discussion, you might find that others in your group have different opinions than yours. That's OK, but each person should be prepared to explain their decision.

After group discussion time, as a whole class, discuss the various responses. Be sure to request the opinions of the high status students. This is an opportunity for all students to hear and learn from them.

Display one situation at a time:

Situation #1
- You walk into the bathroom and see a student who is younger than you picking on an even younger student.

Situation #2
- After school, kids take turns kicking the same student in the behind over and over again.

Situation #3
- At your lunch table someone says Brett can't sit there anymore. Whenever Brett comes to the table, the others spread their arms and legs so there is no room for Brett.

Situation #4
- Casey is a friend of yours. You hear that Toby, an older student, is going to kick Casey's butt after school.

Situation #5
- Brianna is a new student in your school. Your friends keep talking about Brianna having many boyfriends.

Situation #6
- You hear Shea making mean comments to Ronnie, who sits in front of Shea. You have heard Ronnie tell Shea to stop, but Shea continues. You also hear Shea say to Ronnie, "If you tattle, you will get beaten up."

Activity: Tattling vs. Telling

10 This activity is similar to the activity where students discuss how to respond if they witness or know about bullying.

Create groups of three or four students, making sure the students have a chance to get up, move, and work with students with whom they don't usually work. Make sure that the high status students are divided among the groups.

One at a time, write a few of the following scenarios on the board. Ask the students to determine if choosing to talk to an adult about the situation would be tattling or telling. It is acceptable for different students within the group to have different opinions. By the end of the discussion on any particular scenario, make it clear what specific actions *you* expect students to take in a similar situation.

Display one situation at a time:

Situation #1
- You see a weapon in another student's book bag.

Situation #2
- You hear that Colby is going to kick Dakota's butt after school. You can tell that Dakota is afraid.

Situation #3
- You walk into the bathroom as Angel is walking out. You see the sink stuffed with paper and water is over-flowing.

Situation #4
- You become aware that every day Alex steals something out of Jackie's desk. Jackie hasn't noticed anything missing yet.

Situation #5
- On the school bus, you see a student get hit with a spitball. The student turns to a bunch of kids and says, "Cut it out." The kids laugh but don't send anymore spitballs.

Situation #6
- You notice that another student always leaves their garbage on the lunch table and never helps with clean-up.

Situation #7

- You overhear Casey joking at lunch that the teacher is a big, fat fatty.

Situation #8

- You hear a rumor that Lee is going to get rid of all the teachers who really tick him off.

Final Thoughts

Martin Luther King Jr. said, "In the end, we will remember not the words of our enemies, but the silence of our friends." We believe the goal of every school should be to change this quote to the following, "In the end, we will remember not the words of our enemies, but the support of our friends."

Educators must teach students how to respond to bullying. If these lessons are not taught, then we can only hope that as they become adult members of the community they will respond responsibly if they see someone getting mugged, witness child abuse, hear their neighbor's domestic violence, or notice a house or car being vandalized. Hope and luck are not valid bully or crime prevention strategies.

The onus is on the school staff to reinforce and remind students of the expectations if they witness or know about bullying. It is also the responsibility of the school staff to react to information about bullying in a manner that makes it safe for students to talk to an adult about the hurtful behaviors of others. This will create a culture of involvement and an environment of safety.

STATISTICS AND STUDIES

- Six out of ten American teens witness bullying at least once a day. (National Crime Prevention Council, 2003)
- Surprisingly, bullies appear to have little difficulty in making friends. Their friends typically share their pro-violence attitudes and problem behaviors (such as drinking and smoking) and may be involved in bullying as well (Nansel, et al., 2001). These friends are often followers that do not initiate bullying, but participate in it. (Olweus, 1978)
- Classmates of targets do not want to intervene because they fear loss of status or risk being bullied themselves. (Batsche & Knoff, 1994; Charach, Pepler, & Ziegler, 1995)
- Bystanders may be afraid to associate with the victim for fear of lowering their own status or of retribution from the bully and becoming victims themselves; fear reporting bullying incidents because they do not want to be called a "snitch," a "tattler," or an

"informer"; be drawn into bullying behavior by group pressure; feel unsafe, unable to take action or a loss of control. (Shaw, 2003)

- Thirty-nine percent of middle-schoolers and 36 percent of high-schoolers say they don't feel safe at school. (Josephson Institute of Ethics, 2001)
- Playground statistics: Every seven minutes a child is bullied. Adult intervention: 4 percent. Peer intervention: 11 percent. No intervention: 85 percent. (Bullying Statistics, n.d.)

Playful Teasing vs. Hurtful Taunting 8

A friend must not be injured, even in jest.

—SYRUS

Teasing is a playful use of humor that brings people together, lightens a mood, enhances a relationship, and makes people laugh. A funny person who can playfully tease is usually popular and able to maintain healthy friendships. A person can also make others laugh by using humor inappropriately; this is when humor becomes hurtful taunting. When teasing is misused, purposefully or accidentally, problems tend to follow. This lesson will help students understand the difference between playful teasing and hurtful taunting so they can avoid bullying and the expression of disrespectful and insensitive behavior.

We use the words playful teasing and hurtful taunting, but regardless of the words used in your school or community, the focus is to make sure your students understand the difference between good humor and hurtful words.

DEFINING PLAYFUL TEASING VS. HURTFUL TAUNTING

Comments and actions that straddle the line between teasing and taunting are infinite. By teaching the difference between teasing and taunting, misunderstandings can be limited. Misspoken statements will still occur, but they should be the exception, not the rule. Perfection is not the goal, conscientious decision making is.

Materials per student:
paper
pencil

Time: 30 minutes

The difference between playful teasing and hurtful taunting may be obvious to one person but completely missed by another. Until students are taught the difference between teasing and taunting, it is prudent to assume they don't know the difference.

ACTIVITY

1 On the board, write the following phrases:

- "Lighten up. You're too sensitive."
- "I was just kidding."
- "I'm just teasing you."
- "I didn't mean anything by it."
- "Can't you take a joke?"

2 Suggested Script:

Has anyone here ever gotten upset when someone said something hurtful only to hear the other person say any of the following? (Refer to the comments written on the board)

Would you say that you were being overly sensitive or you had good reason to be upset? Allow some of the students to discuss their experiences—remind them not to mention the names of others.

Of course, you are always entitled to your feelings. There are times when any one might be overly sensitive and get upset at someone's remark even when that person really did not mean any harm or want to get you upset. Sometimes people are accidentally mean or insensitive.

On the other hand, sometimes people are purposely mean and they try to hide behind those phrases to protect themselves from being accused of being mean or insensitive. They may act like they weren't trying to hurt your feelings when they really know they did do it on purpose. Instead of apologizing, they tell you that you shouldn't be so sensitive or shouldn't feel insulted—in other words, telling you how you should act or feel. Now they are being mean and controlling. If they were truly sorry, they would apologize without telling you how you should feel. You would know that they were sincere because they would stop making hurtful comments.

Has anyone here ever said something to another person, thinking it was funny, but it turned out to be insulting or rude? Yes, it happens to all of us.

To increase respectful behavior and limit misunderstandings, we are going to learn the difference between teasing and taunting (use the language of your school).

I think having a good sense of humor means being able to make people laugh without hurting anyone's feelings. If someone's feelings are hurt, even though others are laughing, it is not a good use of humor. Let's look at the difference between teasing and taunting:

Note: We suggest you edit our description of playful teasing and hurtful taunting for your students. Have the students write the descriptions on their paper.

Playful teasing can be a good use of humor when it has the following qualities:

- *It isn't intended to hurt the other person.*
- *It's funny in a lighthearted, clever, and gentle way; the comment lightens a mood.*
- *It's stated in a tone of voice that is affectionate.*
- *It is mutual; meant to get both parties to laugh.*
- *It's used to bring people closer together and make the relationship stronger.*
- *It maintains the basic dignity of everyone involved (nobody gets embarrassed or humiliated).*
- *The teasing can go back and forth—not limited to only one person being allowed to make the comments.*
- *It is only a small part of the activities between the people involved—teasing doesn't define the whole relationship.*
- *It stops if someone becomes upset or objects to the comments.*
- *No one gets upset or wants revenge.*

It is hurtful taunting when it has the following qualities:

- *It is intended to upset another.*
- *It is one-sided—one person has a certain power and can make comments, but the other person cannot.*
- *It is mean, humiliating, cruel, demeaning, or bigoted.*
- *It is meant to diminish the self-worth of the target.*
- *It induces fear of further taunting or physical bullying.*
- *It continues even when the targeted person becomes upset or objects to the comments.*
- *It uses an angry, snide, or sarcastic tone of voice.*
- *Bystanders laugh, but not the target(s) of the comment.*
- *Aggressive body language is used—smirking, rolling eyes, raised hip, shaking head back and forth.*

Other phrases to describe teasing and taunting are:
- teasing vs. too much teasing
- playful vs. hurtful
- playing vs. hurting

The line between teasing and taunting is not always clear. Sometimes the fine line between the two is determined by the relationship of the participants.

Even if your intent is to playfully tease someone, there are things to consider so that you can avoid misjudging the situation and hurting someone's feelings. Before you make a comment or attempt humor, consider the following:

- *How well do you know the person?*
- *Has the other person appreciated teasing in the past?*
- *Do you know what subjects are sensitive to the other person?*
- *Is there something going on that would make the other person sensitive to teasing?*
- *Have you and the other person had problems in the past?*
- *What is your relationship to the person? Do you have some sort of power over the person such as age, size, or social status?*
- *Are there gender, race, religion, or other differences that may make some topics off-limits?*

You should not tease a person if you don't know them well, don't get along with them, or know they do not like being teased. To do so under those conditions would be taunting.

If you say or do something with good intentions but find it does hurt someone's feelings, say, "I'm sorry," and avoid repeating the comment or behavior. Do not talk negatively about an offended peer, such as saying to others, "Don't talk to her. She's sooo sensitive." That's a type of taunting.

③ YOU BE THE JUDGE

In the following activity, students discover the difference between teasing and taunting. Use this opportunity to have the students move to a different part of the room and work with students with whom they do not often sit next to or interact with—avoid grouping students with existing conflicts. A potential benefit of this activity is guiding behavior through the use of positive peer pressure. Distribute high status students who know how to use humor respectfully throughout the groups. This is an opportunity for high status students to share what is considered good humor and acceptable teasing with students who use a more cruel sense of humor or purposely taunt. This style of group discussion helps to create empathy as students learn what their peers may feel about an experience.

Create groups of three or four students. Each group will discuss the same scenario. For each scenario, do one of the following, determined by the age and reading ability of your students:

- Write the scenario on the board.
- Write the scenario on a large piece of paper and hang/tape it to the wall so it may be used for another group of students without having to rewrite it.
- Project the scenario onto a screen or wall.

- Write the scenario on paper and hand a copy to each group.
- Say the scenario out loud—more than once.

Suggested Script:

> *Within each group, each of you should share your thoughts and determine if the incident described is playful teasing or hurtful taunting. Each of you should be prepared to talk about your decision both in the group and during the whole class discussion.*

For some students, the intimacy of small group activities increases the chance that they will share their thoughts and feelings.

Peer discussion helps sharpen critical thinking skills and helps your students understand how some may be offended, while others would not be offended in the same or a similar situation.

After discussion within each group, discuss the various responses out loud as a whole class. Ask some high status individuals to share their ideas to take advantage of their influence. This is an opportunity to have the other students hear and learn from them.

Scenario #1: The Whoopee Cushion

Bart moved to town during the middle of the school year and was still trying to make friends. He was thrilled when he was invited to a classmate's birthday party. When everyone sat at the table to cut the birthday cake, someone slid a whoopee cushion on Bart's chair. It made a farting sound when he sat down. Someone jokingly called Bart, "Bart the Fart." Everyone laughed. Bart was embarrassed but laughed along with everyone else.

On Monday morning, one of the kids said, "Hey look, it's Bart the Fart," and everyone laughed. Bart answered, "Hey c'mon, it's not funny anymore," and walked away with his head down. By recess, everyone was calling him "Farty."

Playful teasing or hurtful taunting? Why?

Authors' opinion: Taunting—Once Bart said he didn't think it was funny anymore and expressed distress by walking away with his head down, continuing the comment was taunting.

Scenario #2: Lizard Face

Helena and Roger had been good friends for years. Roger was well known for his interest in lizards. He kept four lizards in a tank in his bedroom and spent a lot of time watching the way they moved. Roger got pretty good at imitating the way lizards stick their tongues out to catch their prey and always got a laugh when he did the "lizard face" in school.

One day, Roger's class was working near the compost pile for their gardening project. On that day, there were a lot of flies hovering around. After a while, one of the kids asked if anyone knew what was being served for lunch. Helena quickly said, "It looks like Lizard Man's lunch is already here. Roger, look at that juicy fly right by your shovel."

Remind the students that respectful discussion means listening to others' ideas even if you don't agree. Put downs and hurtful comments are not acceptable.

Roger laughed along with the other students. A few seconds later Leon piped up and said, "Actually, I think today is pizza day." The kids all said, "Great!" and, "Excellent!"

Playful teasing or hurtful taunting? Why?

Authors' opinion: Teasing—Helena's long friendship with Roger offered the insight that he would not be insulted, and there had been a history of Roger making others laugh with his imitation of lizards. Also, the teasing was momentary, and then the conversation moved on to pizza for lunch.

Scenario #3: Geek Girl

Janet is really good with computers. She loves video games, computer games, and surfing the Internet. She was even working with her cousin to build a computer from scratch. Janet entered a science fair with three friends.

Janet also played sports on the girls' soccer and softball teams. Sometimes the girls would refer to her as, "Computer Chick." She didn't mind, especially when they'd say, "Wow, Computer Chick does it again!" when she'd score a goal or get a big hit. Sometimes Rosie, one of Janet's soccer teammates, called Janet, "Geek Girl." Janet didn't like that nickname, and one day Janet told Rosie that she did not like being called Geek Girl.

Janet's team won a top award at the science fair! They planned a party to celebrate. In secret, her science fair teammates got together and made a special cake for her that looked like a computer. On it they wrote, "To our favorite computer geek. Thanks for all your hard work!"

Playful teasing or hurtful taunting? Why?

Authors' opinion: Discussable—If you assume Janet's science fair teammates did not know Janet did not like being called a geek, and the intent was to show sincere appreciation, then the term "geek" was used in a playful manner, and we would consider it teasing. If her science fair teammates *did* know that Janet did not like being called a geek, using that name would be disrespectful and taunting. According to the scenario, Janet only told Rosie that she didn't like being called a geek, and the science fair teammates may not have known that.

Discussing scenarios in which teasing or taunting is questionable provides students the opportunity to understand how different people interpret situations differently. These discussions encourage an understanding of how others may think or feel about an experience, which helps to increase empathy.

Additional Scenarios

The following scenarios may be used during the initial lesson or to reinforce the teasing or taunting lesson during morning meetings, indoor recess, etc.

Scenario #1: Shaquille's Daughter

Shanti recently moved to town and just finished her first week at her new school. She is at least six inches taller than the next tallest student in her grade. One day, while looking for a place to sit during lunch, another student shouted at her in a mean-spirited way, "Hey, Shorty, you're bigger than Shaquille O'Neal!" Everyone laughed and walked away.

Playful teasing or hurtful taunting? Why?

Scenario #2: Dodge Ball Danny

Your P.E. class is playing dodge ball. Everyone is having fun. All of a sudden Danny runs out in front of his teammates toward the other team, wags his backside and calls out to the other side, "You guys couldn't hit me if your life depended on it."

Playful teasing or hurtful taunting? Why?

Lesson Extension

Don't Ever Tease About . . .

In the following activity students will determine what topics should not be teased about, even with the best of intentions. The activity may be done individually or in groups of two or three.

Write on the board, and have the students write on their paper, the following:

Topics people shouldn't tease about:

* Someone's religion
*
*
*

Suggested Script:

> *Someone's religion or spiritual belief is a topic most people believe others should not tease another person about. Although sometimes it can be done respectfully, it is best to not even attempt it. Your job is to think of other things you think people should not tease about because most people would be sensitive about it and would not appreciate it.*
>
> After an appropriate amount of time, discuss with the students what they believe should be added to the list and write those ideas on the board. Other examples might include:

* Weight
* Body shape
* Race
* Test grades
* Athletic ability

Review your state's harassment law to help determine what topics should be on the list. Refer to http://www.bully police.org.

Lesson Extension

Teaching students to consider the difference between teasing or taunting will help them develop a deeper understanding of respect and empathy, an appropriate sense of humor, and healthy interpersonal relationships. We are guiding students to think before they act. Although we choose to use the words teasing and taunting, our focus is on the concepts behind the words. In that regard, we also want students to understand the difference between bullying or play fighting and flirting or sexual harassment. The following insights extend the discussion about how to determine the difference between teasing and taunting.

Bullying or Play Fighting

Play fighting means that the participants are free to participate, or not, based on their own desires. Play fighting involves positive or neutral facial expressions—see the Emotional Statues activity on page 38. The tone of the voices used or the sounds made by the participants include laughing and other sounds that commonly indicate pleasure.

It is bullying when play fighting continues even though a person is getting hurt or indicates that it is time to stop. Play fighting discontinues when one person says it is time to stop.

Flirting or Sexual Harassment

The concept of flirting or sexual harassment is usually reserved for older students. However, romantic interest or harassment based on sexuality can begin quite early. Parents and teachers together need to determine when it is appropriate to address this concept. We offer the following view on the difference between flirting and sexual harassment:

Flirting is a reciprocal interaction between two people. Flirting is flattering or complimentary and is appreciated. Flirting boosts self-esteem and makes one feel good or special.

Sexual harassment is demeaning. It is unwanted, one-sided, and involves degrading and disrespectful words or actions. With harassment, the receiver feels powerless, humiliated, or embarrassed (similar to the definition of bullying). Harassment is harmful, vindictive, and cruel. It is also illegal.

Final Thoughts

By playing out various scenarios, the line between teasing and taunting becomes clearer. Regardless of the words used in your school or community, playful teasing brings people together, and hurtful taunting drives people apart. Learning how to use humor appropriately is a difficult lesson for some students. When they make a mistake they will need a friendly reminder from a staff member to clarify how to use humor to create positive feelings and include others.

STATISTICS AND STUDIES

- Seventy-four percent of eight- to eleven-year-old students said teasing and bullying occur at their schools. (Kaiser Family Foundation and Nickelodeon, 2001)
- Regarding verbal bullying, bullies were less likely to make derogatory statements about other students' religion or race. "There seem to be stronger social norms against making these kinds of statements than against belittling someone about their appearance or behavior." (Nansel, et al., 2001)
- ". . . when the teasing turns to taunting and the child is afraid that any attempt to stop the aggressor will cause harm, the situation is more serious and possibly crosses the line into bullying." (Puhl & Latner, 2007)
- Taunts, shoves, and social isolation can wreak emotional and physical harm in childhood and possibly beyond that is distinct from the health consequences of being overweight. (Puhl & Latner, 2007)
- Bullying and teasing are cited as the top school troubles of students ages eight to fifteen. (The Kaiser Family Foundation)

Making Friends 9

Strategies to Resist Social Aggression

> *When one door of happiness closes, another opens; but often we look so long at the closed door that we do not see the one which has been opened for us.*
>
> —HELEN KELLER

DEFINITION OF SOCIAL AGGRESSION

! Any act in which a relationship is used as a weapon, including manipulation, silent treatment, targeting social status, rumor spreading, and "do (or don't do) this and I won't be your friend."

Social aggression is using the power of a social group to abuse and hurt others. Social aggression is about keeping a targeted person out of a desired social group, i.e., social isolation. Why? Because someone, or a group, decides that keeping that person out is to their advantage. Often, the targeted person is someone who had been part of the group—someone with whom there had been a friendship. Social aggression is arguably the most common type of bullying; pervasive, yet easy to overlook and often ignored by adults.

The view that boys fight it out and then are friends again is inaccurate. Although there is some truth to this perspective, it usually relates to arguments between boys who are somewhat equal to each other, not a bully and a target.

135

Social aggression is the type of bullying most commonly attributed to girls and is sometimes referred to as girl bullying. The most common reason for this description is that it has not been traditionally acceptable for girls to fight or be blatantly mean—girls have been expected to be ladylike and friendly toward everyone. In the not too distant past, if a girl didn't like another girl or desired to attain power or influence over another, she had to act covertly. This style of bullying still exists and is used by both girls and boys. Social aggression is not limited to girls, just as physical bullying is not limited to boys.

Fortunately, in modern culture, girls have more freedom to be physical and athletic, without losing their femininity. This, in turn, may limit their vulnerability to social aggression.

A few years ago I was talking about social aggression with one of my two sons. My son was in middle school, and I asked him to critique a presentation on social aggression that I was preparing. He listened and then said: "Dad, why do you say that girls are mostly affected by social aggression or do more social aggression? I know plenty of boys in my school who manipulate, gossip, and leave people out. It's not just a girl problem. It bothers guys, too." I'm glad I asked an expert in the field. He was absolutely right.—MD

Human beings are social creatures. We want and need friends and acceptance into the larger community. For some people, the desire for friends and acceptance is so great they will continue relationships even if their friends treat them poorly. It is this strong desire for friendship and acceptance that makes someone vulnerable to social aggression.

The trap in social aggression is that the aggressor(s) is usually someone in a person's social group and therefore harder to ignore or stay away from. A person who has been kicked out of their social group and has no other group to go to will find themselves alone and very lonely. They feel left out, wondering, "What did I do wrong?" and, "What can I do to belong to the group again?" Ideally, targets of social aggression should look for another group to befriend. Targets remain targets when they focus on where they are not wanted, instead of thinking about where they can be appreciated.

Children without any obvious skills or tangible accomplishments are at greater risk of direct bullying and social aggression.

LIKES AND YIKES—DETERMINING FRIENDSHIP QUALITIES

This lesson begins with a discussion about the importance of friendships in our lives. Earlier, students learned how to deal with people who treat them badly. But what do you do if you have a mean friend?

Materials
per group:
8½ × 11 paper
pencil

Time: 45–60 minutes

GOAL: Students will decide what qualities they want in a friend and what qualities they will not tolerate.

ACTIVITY

On the board write, "I have a mean friend."

1 Suggested Script:

What exactly does, "I have a mean friend" mean? Solicit responses from students. Then say, *Friends should not be mean. If someone is consistently mean, they should not be considered a friend. However, friends do makc mistakes, express unpleasant moods, and disagree with us. But even at those times, friends still treat each other with respect.*

Since friends are so important, we are going to spend some time thinking about what qualities people want in a friend.

What are the qualities that are important to you? Put three responses on the board. Discuss the responses. Some qualities, such as truthful, clean, and honest don't need clarification. However, if subjective qualities, such as respectful, nice, or friendly come up, ask for a specific example.

Friends are not mean. If they do something mean it should be the exception, not the rule.

2 Create groups of four to six students. Each group will brainstorm and write a list of eight to twelve qualities they want in a friend. This list will be a longer version of what you already have begun on the board.

3 After the group creates a list of desirable qualities, have each individual in the group decide the top three qualities from the list that are most important to them. Have each person put a check mark on the list next to the three qualities they value the most. After each person in the group has made their check marks, have one of the group members circle the three qualities that received the most votes.

Figure 9.1 shows an example of a student-generated list with check marks and the most popular qualities circled.

4 As the students are doing this work, draw a big circle on the board like the one shown in Figure 9.2 below. Inside the circle, draw a person with a happy face. This does not have to be a masterpiece. A stick figure with a big head featuring a happy face will do just fine.

Figure 9.1

Friendship Likes
1) clean
2) active ✔
3) fun ✔
4) sense of humor ✔✔✔
5) attractive ✔
6) loyal ✔✔✔
7) smart ✔
8) nice
9) similar interests ✔✔✔
10) respectful ✔✔

If a student is struggling to think of desirable qualities, ask the student to think of qualities they have that make them a good friend.

Figure 9.2

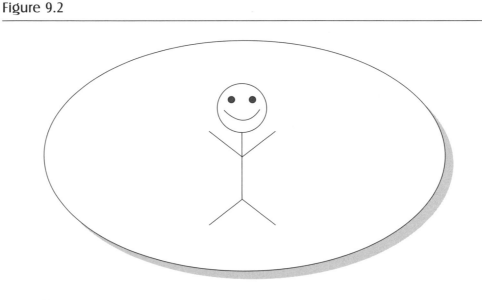

5 When the students have completed their assignment, ask each group what they chose as the top three qualities of a friend. Write these responses down within the boundaries of the circle you drew on the board, as shown in Figure 9.3. If a quality is repeated among different groups, make extra check marks next to that quality indicating that this quality came up more than once.

Remember, ask the students to articulate specifically why they desire these qualities and avoid one-word answers.

The responses within the circle are within the personal boundary and are called "Likes."

Figure 9.3

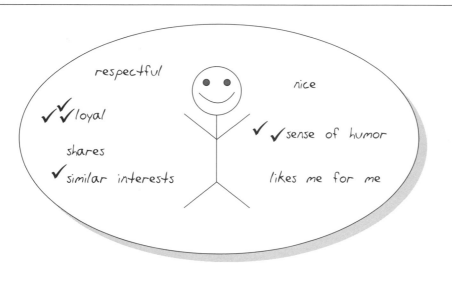

Remember that the Likes qualities being discussed are from the students' point of view. Although you may not think cute or rich are important qualities for a friendship, your students are just learning. If these kinds of qualities show up in the Likes section, add them to the inner circle. Then, in a nonjudgmental way, ask the students to explain why these qualities are important to them and discuss their answers.

One time, in a fifth-grade class, rich was one of the qualities that one group determined as important. I asked them, "What if a friend of yours had all these other qualities, such as caring, shares, loyal, and fun, but you found out the family was actually very poor?" One of the students quickly stated, "Well, I mean rich in humor, rich in intelligence, and rich in generosity." I thought it was more quick thinking than what was originally meant, but I said, "Oh. I see. In fact, I agree with you." I believe the whole class got the point, the group saved face, and I didn't come off as preachy or judgmental.

—SB

"YIKES!"

6 The next part of the activity is similar to the first, except this time ask for qualities that the students will not accept in a friendship. Explain that you are not talking about one-time mistakes. For instance, if someone calls you a mean name and you tell that person that it bothers you and the name calling stops, then you can continue to be friends. But if name-calling continues, you should reconsider the friendship.

You might find that some people struggle with brainstorming in this part of the activity. If this is the case, ask them to consider the opposite of what they wrote for Likes.

After the group creates a list of undesirable qualities, have each individual in the group decide the top three unacceptable qualities from the list—the three worst of the worst. Have each person put a check mark on the list next to the three qualities they dislike most. After each person in the group has made their check marks, have one of the group members circle the three qualities that received the most votes. After the groups finish selecting their top three unacceptable qualities in a friend, write their responses on the outside of the circle that you had drawn on the board as in Figure 9.4. As you did with the Likes, flesh out those words that need more specific discussion such as, "What do you mean by abusive?" and, "What does too jealous mean?"

Figure 9.4

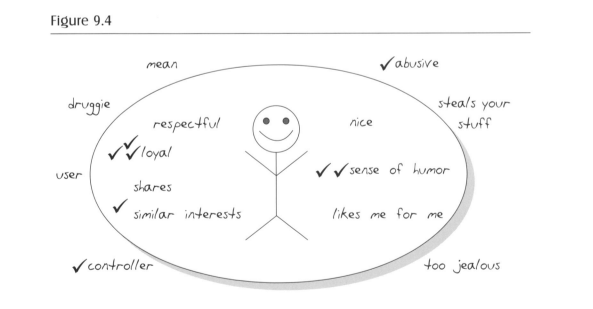

7 Wrap up the lesson by asking the students, *"If you want friends with the qualities you have listed inside the circle, what kind of qualities do you have to have?"* "You have to have the Likes qualities," is the answer we always receive. Remind the students that the Likes and

Yikes qualities were not created by teachers or parents. The qualities listed are the values of this class.

8 Post a copy of the Likes and Yikes results where the students line up so they may refer to it often.

Final Thoughts

When an adult considers making a large purchase, such as a car or house, they offer something of great value in return; their hard-earned money. Before purchasing, many adults research and consider the pros and cons of such an investment. Some of your students may already engage in similar behavior when they consider buying something important such as a computer, music player, bicycle, or a dirt bike. Your students are also making a big investment when developing and maintaining friendships. It is an investment not of cash, but of trust and of oneself. In close friendships, individuals share secrets, thoughts, feelings, fantasies, dreams, and desires while feeling cared for and respected.

PERSONAL BOUNDARIES

The line separating the qualities determined in the Likes and Yikes activity represents a personal boundary. This activity will help students clarify their personal boundaries and recognize the danger signs that indicate people with Yikes qualities are trying to cross, or have crossed, their personal boundary.

Materials:
Three bandanas
or colored
index cards:
one green,
one yellow,
one red

> **GOAL: Students will clarify their personal boundaries and identify when their boundaries have been crossed.**

Time: 20 minutes

ACTIVITY

Personal Boundaries

Note regarding materials: Do not let the students know that you have the bandanas or index cards. Before the lesson starts, put each differently colored bandana or card in a different pocket. Or, put them all in one pocket, red at the bottom, yellow in the middle, and green at top (the first to come out). If you put the bandanas or cards in the same pocket, make sure they come out one at a time, in the correct order.

1 Create a space in the room so that one person can stand in the middle and four more participants can surround that person by standing in each corner of an imaginary square (the square doesn't have to be exact). Each participant should be about fifteen feet away from the volunteer in the middle.

2 Choose a volunteer who you believe is aware of and enforces their personal boundaries. For this explanation, we will call that person Vonnie.

1. Ask Vonnie to identify a friend in the room.

2. Ask Vonnie to pick another student in the room—someone who Vonnie *does not know* very well.

3. Randomly choose a third student—an acquaintance of Vonnie, certainly no one with whom there is tension.

4. You will be the fourth person in the demonstration. You and the three other people in the demonstration with Vonnie will be referred to as "participants."

5. Have Vonnie stand in the middle of the created space. The other four participants, including you, will surround Vonnie by standing in each corner of an imaginary square. (See Figure 9.5)

Figure 9.5

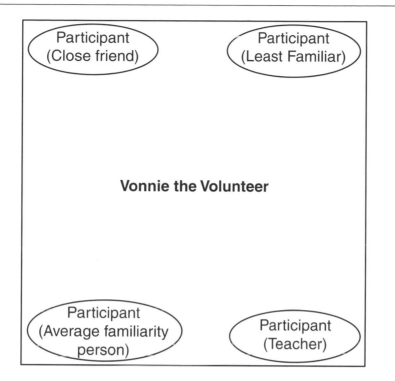

 Suggested Script:

I will say the name of each participant one at a time. When I say a participant's name, that person will walk slowly toward Vonnie. When Vonnie feels that the participant has walked close enough for Vonnie's comfort—be it 2 feet or 14½ feet—Vonnie will say, "Stop," and the participant will stop walking. Each participant will stay at that spot as the next participant is called and performs the same action.

Begin by calling the name of the first participant. You will be the last participant to walk toward Vonnie.

4 After all participants have walked toward Vonnie, point out the difference between how close each person was allowed to get to Vonnie (see Figure 9.6). Most likely, the people who Vonnie knows best, and feels comfortable with, will be physically closer than those people with whom Vonnie has less experience, trust, or comfort. Ask Vonnie, *"Why are some people allowed to be closer to you than others?"*

Figure 9.6

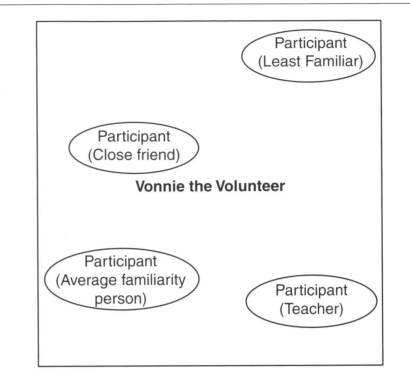

5 *"Vonnie, what do you think it would take to allow a person who you don't know very well to stand a bit closer to you?"* The response and ensuing discussion should include the following criteria: "If a person continues to show respect and both people want to develop a closer friendship, in time they would be allowed to come closer." Most students will not be this articulate but will attempt to express a similar concept. Use this opportunity to help them clarify and articulate these thoughts.

"We all have personal boundaries. For instance, you all identified some of your personal boundaries when you decided what qualities you value in a friend and what qualities you will not accept."

Ask the students to return to their seats.

6 Request another volunteer for a similar demonstration as the first. Pick a volunteer with whom you are comfortable, but do not have a very close relationship. Again, we'll use the name Vonnie as the name of the volunteer. This time *you* will be the only person walking toward Vonnie.

7 Stand about fifteen feet from Vonnie. Say to Vonnie, *"I will walk toward you and you should say, "Stop," when I am close enough for your comfort."* Begin to slowly walk toward Vonnie.

When Vonnie says, "Stop," stop walking and state that you respect the boundary. Take out and wave the green card or bandana. Say, *"Like a traffic light, green means go and if you see that a person respects your boundary, then, if you so choose, you can 'go' ahead with the friendship."*

8 Step back to your starting spot and begin again, reminding Vonnie to say stop when appropriate. This time, when Vonnie says, "Stop," keep walking closer. Expect that Vonnie will say, "Stop," again and this time stop even if Vonnie does not repeat the request to stop or quietly steps back from your advance. With a sincere tone say, *"Oh, I'm sorry, I didn't realize you said stop. I apologize."* Take a couple of steps back.

Pull out and wave the yellow card or bandana. Say, *"Yellow means caution. Sometimes people make mistakes, and when they do, you should be cautious—especially at the beginning of a new friendship. They have not yet proven that they respect your boundaries. You may consider continuing the friendship if you believe they will respect your boundaries in the future."*

9 Step back to your starting spot and begin a third time, reminding Vonnie to say, "Stop," when Vonnie wants you to stop. This time, when Vonnie says, "Stop," keep going . . . and going . . . and going. Expect Vonnie to show signs of nervousness, uncertainty, and that Vonnie will either continue to repeat, "Stop," (perhaps even louder) or will back off from your nearing presence. Finally, take a step back and pull out the red card or bandana.

Suggested Script:

> *Red means STOP! When a person purposefully and continuously disrespects you, you need to enforce your personal boundaries by assertively stating your boundaries or by ending the friendship.*
>
> *When someone clearly does something you don't like, such as bullying you, your boundary has been crossed—a red flag has been raised. This person has to stop bullying you, or you have to end the friendship and find a new friend. Remember, real friends respect all your personal boundaries by respecting your body, feelings, and belongings.*

Final Thoughts

This lesson is a tangible way for students to understand the importance of being aware of personal boundaries. Use some of the qualities from the Likes and Yikes activity (page 136) to discuss how friends show respect, or disrespect, in regard to personal boundaries. Confirm that students understand respecting personal boundaries is not only physical, but emotional as well.

Using someone's property without permission is an example of not respecting someone's boundaries. This could be forgiven if the action is not repeated.

Continually disrespecting a personal boundary is an example of what people mean when they say, "That's a major red flag."

You can't control others, but you can control whether or not you allow someone to repeatedly disrespect you.

Once a student is aware of their personal boundaries, they can enforce those boundaries. Of course, sometimes a person may find that the only way to enforce their boundaries is by ending a friendship. Students need new friends to lessen vulnerability to social aggression and to avoid keeping a mean friend. How and where to find new friends is discussed in the next lesson.

FINDING NEW FRIENDS

Making friends is difficult for some people. This lesson helps students identify their own interests and use these interests to identify new places to look for potential friends. The idea is to look within before looking around.

Suggestions for making new friends usually include becoming involved in various activities, smiling, being upbeat, being yourself, fitting in, expressing confidence, being polite, and listening to and showing interest in others. These suggestions are valid and for people who already have these qualities, making friends can be easy and appear effortless. For others, these concepts are ambiguous, and making friends is very challenging and quite intimidating. It is especially difficult for people who are new to an environment, have low self-esteem, or lack abilities and social skills. Students who have difficulty making or maintaining healthy friendships need the direct assistance of parents, teachers, and other trusted adults in creating opportunities and developing skills to make friends.

Most people prefer good friends over bad friends, but many people will choose bad friends over no friends at all.

Personal Interest Inventory

Materials:
one copy of the
    Personal Interest
    Inventory for
    each student
    (see page 149)
pencil for each student

GOAL: Students will identify their interests and hobbies.

Time: 20 minutes

ACTIVITY

1 Before beginning the suggested script, ask the students to remind you of the qualities they desire in a friendship.

Suggested Script:

> *As we discussed, you may find that some people you spend time with may bully you and display other Yikes qualities. Although you may tell the person to stop, they may not change their behavior. Therefore, you need to change who you are spending time with. That can be difficult if you don't have other friends to choose from. You will need to look for other people who you can be friends with; people with Likes qualities who will respect your personal boundaries.*
>
> *How does one go about finding people to be friends with? Where does one look? The answer lies within you. A good place to start is to look for others who have similar interests. Therefore, we are going to do an activity so that each of you can identify your own interests and hobbies.*

Be the type of person you want to have as a friend.

2 After handing out the Personal Interest Inventory, instruct the students:

- *You do not have to go in order.*
- *If uncertain of an answer, come back to it later and answer it.*
- *You may write more than one interest in each space.*
- *For this activity, lunch and recess are not subjects in school.*

3 Sharing the information:

1. After the students have filled in their papers, explain that you want to know what the students in this class are interested in.

2. Instruct the students to stand if they wrote something similar on their paper to what you are about to say. For instance, the first sentence on the Personal Interest Inventory is, *My favorite subject in school is _____ (blank). Stand if you wrote "science."*

3. Ask the students to look around the room to see who stands for each answer. Remind them that this activity will provide clues as to who has similar interests and who might make good prospective friends.

4. Give a few answers for each sentence so that most students have an opportunity to stand.

After the Personal Interest Inventory is completed, suggest to your students that they take the Personal Interest Inventory home and store it in a special place so at some future date they can see how much their interests have changed or remained the same.

 Any of the Personal Interest Inventory sentences can be deleted, changed, or have new sentences added.

Visit our website at http://www.BalanceEducationalServices.com to download a Microsoft Word copy of the Personal Interest Inventory. Use this download to print out copies or use as a template to make changes that fit your needs.

Final Thoughts

The Personal Interest Inventory indicates a student's interest in activities and hobbies such as sports, music, theater, computer games, and crafts. Adults working with a student who has few friends or is a target can use the Personal Interest Inventory to gauge the student's interest level in various activities. Help the student access others who are interested in the same activities. As necessary, adults should provide skills training—physical skills and social skills—to bring them up to a level that will be appreciated by their peers.

STATISTICS AND STUDIES

- Bullying generally begins in the elementary grades, peaks in the sixth through eighth grades, and persists into high school. (Ericson, 2001)
- Research shows that those who bully and are bullied appear to be at greatest risk of experiencing the following: loneliness; trouble making friends; lack of success in school; and involvement in problem behaviors such as smoking and drinking. (Ericson, 2001)
- Boys generally harm others with physical or verbal aggression because this behavior is consistent with the physical dominance peer group goals of boys. Girls, on the other hand, are more apt to focus their aggression on relational issues with their peers. This behavior is consistent with the social peer group and intimacy goals of girls. This kind of aggression is more characteristic of girls, though not exclusive to girls, and is done with the

intention of damaging another child's friendship or feelings of inclusion within a social group. (Crick & Grotpeter, 1995)

- There appears to be a strong relationship between bullying other students and experiencing later legal and criminal problems as an adult. In one study, 60 percent of those characterized as bullies in grades 6–9 had at least one criminal conviction by age twenty-four (Olweus, 1993). Chronic bullies seem to maintain their behaviors into adulthood, negatively influencing their ability to develop and maintain positive relationships. (Oliver, Hoover, & Hazler, 1994)

- Bullies and victims of bullying have difficulty adjusting to their environments, both socially and psychologically. Victims of bullying have greater difficulty making friends and are lonelier. (Nansal, et al., 2001)

- One study found that the most frequent reason cited by youth for persons being bullied is that they "didn't fit in." (Oliver, & Hazler, 1992)

Personal Interest Inventory
A strategy to assist in making friends

Name_____ Date_____

1. My favorite subject in school is_____.

2. My favorite season is _____. In this season I like to _____.

3. An activity I like to do indoors is _____.

4. An activity I like to do outdoors is _____.

5. When I am with my family I like to_____.

6. When I am with other people I like to _____.

7. An activity I have not tried and would like to try is
   _____.

8. An activity I have done and would like to do more is
   _____.

9. When I get older, I think I might like to become a
   _____.

10. A possible place to meet other people like me is
    _____.

Unit Test
Chapters 7, 8, 9

What is a bystander?

_____

_____

_____

List five positive behaviors a bystander can do when they witness bullying.

_____

_____

_____

_____

_____

If you receive a mean e-mail or an IM about someone else, what should you do? Circle the correct answers:

- Ignore it
- Write a mean e-mail or IM about the person who sent it to you
- Delete it
- Send the e-mail or IM to all of your best friends
- Show the e-mail or IM to a trusted adult
- Do not send the e-mail or IM to anyone else

True or False:

_____ Tattling is when a person tells about the actions of another for the purpose of getting that person in trouble. It is tattling if no one and nothing is in danger or will be in danger.

_____ Telling is when a person tells another person in authority that someone or something is getting hurt, or might get hurt, either physically or emotionally. A person who is telling is trying to help a person or a thing.

_____ An example of tattling is telling the teacher Phil shares his lunch with George.

_____ An example of telling is letting an adult know that two people are fighting in the hall.

_____ It is telling if you let an adult know that someone is being hurt.

List three examples of playful teasing.

_____

_____

_____

List three examples of hurtful taunting.

_____

_____

_____

Multiple Choice: Circle the correct answer:
If you want friends with a certain set of qualities, what kind of qualities do you have to have?

1. Similar qualities.

2. The exact opposite qualities.

3. No qualities at all.

What is a personal boundary?

_____

_____

_____

If a friend keeps disrespecting your personal boundaries, what should you do? Circle the correct answers:
- Threaten to hit him or her.
- Ask that person to stop doing the thing that is bothering you.
- Stop hanging out with that person.
- Get another friend to hurt them.
- Spread lies about that person.
- That person is your friend—allow him or her to disrespect your boundaries.

**Final Test
For Chapters 1–9**

Write an example of respectful behavior.

_____

The following are five steps of problem solving and conflict resolution. Using the numbers 1, 2, 3, 4, and 5, list the proper order.

_____ Decide Plan "A"
_____ Weigh the "Pros" and "Cons" of each idea
_____ Brainstorm ideas
_____ Define the Problem or Conflict
_____ Decide Backup Plan "B"

Circle all the ideas that are healthy ways to calm down:
• biting your lip until it bleeds
• kicking a soccer ball
• drawing
• writing your thoughts and feelings in a journal
• talking to someone you trust
• punching a wall
• exercising
• yelling at someone smaller than you

There are five qualities to assertiveness. Put a check mark next to each.
_____ making eye contact
_____ being smart
_____ being calm and in control
_____ using a neutral tone of voice
_____ being very tall
_____ saying what you want
_____ having money
_____ having big muscles
_____ waving your arms
_____ being cute
_____ yelling
_____ using strong body language

Why is communicating assertively useful?

_____

_____

_____

List the Bully Proofing Plan of Action.

_____

_____

_____

** Severity clause: Protect your body at all times.

List five positive behaviors a bystander can do when they witness bullying.

_____

_____

_____

_____

_____

Epilogue

We hope the activities and lessons in this book help your students develop the skills needed for healthy and well-balanced relationships in all areas of their lives. They are designed to be effective and fun ways of teaching the skills that are required by state curriculum and to help children navigate through life's challenges.

Empathy, respect, and other skills needed for healthy friendships do not just occur, nor is there a one-size-fits-all program to teach these skills to our students. Social skills need to be reviewed, discussed, practiced, and role modeled throughout the school year. In addition, students who consistently misbehave will need extra practice to develop pro-social behaviors. We also suggest seeking other lessons and activities, besides those contained in this book, as a way to keep pro-social lessons new, fresh, and interesting for your students. In return, your students will be more empathetic and inclusive, creating a classroom atmosphere where everyone is free to learn.

In closing, as you teach these lessons, remember to have fun.

—Steve, Michael, and Karen

Resources

RESOURCE A
Problems and Conflicts to Resolve

1. Others won't let you join the soccer game (or basketball, football, etc.).	2. You want to use the swings, but they are all occupied.
3. A partner in your group project is not doing the work they are supposed to do.	4. Kids on top of the playground bars won't make room for you or let you up.
5. You put a lot of effort into drawing a picture and someone laughed at it.	6. Someone is saying bad things about one of your family members.

7. Someone keeps calling you an insulting name.

8. Friends won't share the ball or the jump rope with you.

9. A group of kids tells you that you cannot sit at their lunch table.

10. Someone messed up your nice shirt or pants.

11. Someone keeps making fun of the way you look.

12. A person in the car is smoking and it is bothering you.

13. You want to go to the movies but your friend wants to go to the mall.

14. You want to sleep over at a friend's house. Your parents say no.

15. Friends are doing things that you don't think are healthy (smoking, hanging out with a rough crowd, snorting sugar, using inhalants, etc.).

16. Someone keeps sending you nasty e-mails or IMs (instant messages).

17. A friend is saying hurtful things about another friend of yours.

18. You have been invited to two different parties on the same night.

19. You are invited to join a fun game with friends, but the friend you are with is not invited.

20. A classmate rolls their eyes when you speak during class.

RESOURCE B
Assertive Statements

1. Thank you for asking, but I do not want to play right now.

2. Please do not speak to me like that.

3. Thank you, but I do not like broccoli.

4. I am very tired. I don't want to be teased right now.

5. I would rather not hang out with those people. Let's do something else.

6. I don't think it's the right thing to do and I don't want to do it.

7. I don't want to do that. But let's see if we can compromise.

8. Please do not play with my things.

9. If you are going to play with my toys, please put them away when you are finished.

10. For my birthday I would like to receive a video game.

11. I want pizza for dinner. Thank you for asking.

12. Thank you for asking, but I am not interested in going to that party.

13. I'm in a bad mood today. I would like to spend the day by myself.

14. Please don't interrupt when I am talking.

15. I don't like movies like that. Let's find one that we both like.

16. I like you a lot, but I don't like when you tease me.

17. How about spaghetti tonight, and tomorrow we will have sandwiches?

18. I can't talk on the phone now. I'll see you tomorrow.

19. That's cheating, but I would be happy to help you study.

20. That embarrasses me. Please don't do that in front of other people.

21. Thank you, but I was told not to talk to strangers.

22. I have a headache; I would rather just take a nap. But thank you for asking.

23. When you don't ask my opinion, it makes me feel unimportant.

24. I really like you, but I don't like the decision you made.

25. Excuse me. I was in line first. Please don't go in front of me.

26. I need to finish this job. I will be happy to help you when I am finished.

27. That sounds great, but I've got other plans this weekend.

28. Let's all play together.

29. Can my friend join in?

30. Let's let the younger kids play.

31. Let's make room so Taylor can sit here, too.

32. Please stop making faces at me. I don't like it.

33. Can I play too?

34. Leave my backpack alone.

35. That's my spot in line.

36. Excuse me. Would you please move your papers over to your part of the table?

37. Do you want to go to the movies on Saturday?

38. Do you want to go skiing with me next weekend?

39. Excuse me, where is the bathroom?

40. Maybe we can get together another time.

41. May I borrow your pencil?

42. May I pet your dog?

43. Let's not talk about other people when they're not here.

RESOURCE C

Assertive Communication Scenarios

1. Someone steps in front of you in the lunch line.

2. You are hanging out with some people. A couple of them light up a cigarette and ask you if you want to smoke. You do not want to.

3. Your friend keeps making comments to you during a movie or a TV show.

4. Your parent asks you to do a chore, but your favorite show is about to start.

5. Someone taunts you about a body part, and you don't like it.

6. Your brother or sister has been using the computer for a long time and you would like to use it.

7. Your sibling is on the computer IMing about "stuff." You need the computer for a homework assignment, and it is getting late.

8. A teacher accuses you of something you did not do.

9. You believe a former friend is saying nasty things about you to other people.

10. A friend invites themself to sleep over, and you would rather they wouldn't.

11. You are eating dinner at a friend's house, and they serve you something you really don't like.

12. You are spending the night with friends, and someone suggests you raid the parent's liquor cabinet.

13. Your teacher gives you a poor grade on an essay test. You feel it was unfair.

14. Your parent is serving the same food three nights in a row. You didn't like it the first two nights, and definitely don't want it tonight.

15. Your mom goes to give you a hug and kiss in front of all your friends, and you are embarrassed.

16. Your friend calls you a nickname you don't like.

17. You come home from school and find that your younger brother or sister played with a game of yours that was in your room and is supposed to be off-limits.

18. Your brother or sister left your magazine outside, and it got ruined when it rained.

19. A bunch of other students are saying things to another student and causing them to cry. This is really bothering you.

20. Your friends want to see a movie you know your parents would not approve of, and you want to respect your parents' wishes.

RESOURCE D

Lesson Outlines

Chapter 1
"Same Page" Understanding of Violence, Respect, and Bullying

Lesson Outline
Defining Violence

Materials: a one-liter water bottle filled with water (or similar size object), adult volunteer

1. Discuss the definition of violence. Step 1, Page 3

2. Have a student volunteer join you in front of the class. Pretend to hit the student. Ask the class, *"If I hit someone, is it violence?"* Solicit responses. End the discussion clarifying that the answer is, *"Yes, it is violence because it fits the definition of violence."* Step 2, Page 3

3. Call up another volunteer. Pretend to throw an object at the volunteer. Ask the class, *"If I purposely throw something at someone and hit them, is it violence?"* Solicit responses. End the discussion by clarifying that the answer is yes because someone might get hurt or feel intimidated. Step 3, Page 4

4. Demonstrate how to appropriately throw an object to another person. Step 3, Page 4

5. Call up a third volunteer. Pretend to throw an object near the volunteer. Ask the class, *"Is it violence if I throw something near someone to scare them, but purposely miss?"* Solicit responses. End the discussion by clarifying that the answer is yes because it was meant to scare, threaten, or intimidate. Step 4, Page 5

6. Ask an adult to act as the target or use an inanimate object. **Do not use a student volunteer.** Pretend to verbally threaten the adult volunteer. Turn to the students and ask, *"Was that violence?"* Solicit responses. End the discussion by clarifying that the answer is yes because of the threat of violence. Step 5, Page 6

7. Stand far from the adult volunteer. In a soft tone, insult the adult volunteer. Ask the class, *"Was that violence?"* Solicit responses. End the discussion by clarifying that such behavior is unacceptable. Step 6, Page 6

Lesson Outline
What is Bullying and Respect?

Materials: paper, pencil, dictionary

1. Discuss the definition of bullying and the different styles of bullying: physical, verbal, relational (a.k.a. social aggression) and cyber. Step 1, Page 8

2. Discuss the definition of respect and give examples. Step 2 and Step 3, Pages 9–10

3. On the board, draw the Respect, Disrespect, Bullying chart. Step 4, see example on Page 10

4. Have the students create the chart on their paper. Step 4, Page 10

5. Ask the students to write two or three new examples of respect, disrespect, and bullying in the appropriate columns. Step 4, Page 10

6. Count off 1, 2, 3, 1, 2, 3, etc., so every student is a number 1, 2, or 3. Step 5, Page 10

7. As indicated by their assigned numbers and the corresponding column on the chart, have students write their examples on the board. Step 6, Pages 10–11

8. Review the students' examples of respect, disrespect, and violence. Step 7, Page 11

Lesson Outline
Ground Rules

Materials per student: one half-sheet of letter-size paper

1. Hand out a half-sheet of standard letter-size paper, pencil. Step 1, Page 12

2. Explain the concept of the term "ground rules." Step 1, Page 12

3. Write on the board, "**Ground Rules**: I will not hurt: 1. **Myself.** Discuss examples of how a person should not hurt themselves, including physically, verbally, emotionally, and psychologically, etc. Step 1, Page 12

4. Add to the list, "2. **Others.**" Discuss examples of how a person should not hurt others. Step 2, Page 13

5. Add to the list, "3. **Animals.**" Discuss examples of how a person should not hurt animals. Discuss the difference between abusing and hunting. Step 3, Page 13

6. Add to the list, "4. **Property.**" Discuss examples of how a person should not destroy property that is of value to someone. Step 4, Page 14

Optional
Have the students fold up the paper and put it in their shoe for later discussion with family.

Activity: Property or Not Property
Have the students come up with their own lists of things that some might consider valuable and others might consider junk.

Chapter 2
Solving Problems Peacefully and Resolving Conflicts Respectfully

Lesson Outline
The Five Steps of Solving Problems Peacefully
and Resolving Conflicts Respectfully

Materials per group: 8½ × 11 paper, pencil, conflict cards (See Resource A)

1. Discuss the importance of learning how to solve problems peacefully and resolve conflicts respectfully. Step 1, Page 19

2. Describe the soccer scenario to your students. Step 2, Page 20

3. On the board, write the five steps of conflict resolution. Step 3, Pages 20–26
    1. Define the problem or conflict
    2. Brainstorm ideas
    3. Weigh the "Pros" and "Cons" of each idea
    4. Decide Plan "A"
    5. Decide Backup Plan "B"

4. Explain and implement each step in relation to the scenario. Teach the physical reminders. Step 3, Pages 20–26

5. Ask a few students what they would choose as a Plan "A" and a Plan "B." Step 4, Page 26

6. Divide the class into groups of three to four students. In each group assign a scribe to write down the ideas and pros and cons. Step 5, Pages 26–29

7. Hand out a conflict card to each group. Step 5, Pages 26–29

8. Remind the students about respecting others' brainstorming ideas. Step 5, Pages 26–29

9. Discuss each group's solutions. Step 5, Pages 26–29

Chapter 3
Creating Empathy

Lesson Outline
What Makes You Feel...?

Materials: paper, pencil

1. Define empathy. Step 1, Page 32

2. On the board write, "What makes you feel . . ." Step 2, Pages 32–33

3. Ask the students to write their answers to the following questions. Step 2, Pages 32–33

4. Under "What makes you feel . . . ," say and write emotion words such as happy, mad, sad, etc. Step 2, Pages 32–33

5. Discuss some of the students' answers. Step 3, Page 33

    Lesson Extension: List of emotion words, Page 34–36

    Lesson Extension: Find Emotion Words, Page 37

    Lesson Extension: Word Scramble, Page 38

Lesson Outline
Emotional Statues

Materials: none

1. Explain that people communicate emotions through "body language." Explain to the students that they will be doing an activity called "Emotional Statues" and they are going to walk around the room respectfully. Step 1, Page 39

2. Explain the rules of "Emotional Statues": when you call out an emotion word, the students will turn toward the middle of the room and strike a pose portraying that emotion. Step 2, Page 39

3. Demonstrate an example of an emotional statue and explain the physical details of your pose. Step 2, Page 39

4. Have the students walk around the room. Call out an emotion word. Describe the differences you see in how different students physically express the same emotion. Step 3, Pages 39–40

5. Have the students face the center of the room. Tell a story using emotion words. When each emotion word is said, the students will become an emotional statue of that word. Step 4, Page 40

6. Describe a one-sentence situation without indicating an emotion word. Each student will express their own emotional statue based on their feeling about the situation. Describe the details of your students' emotional statues. Step 5, Pages 40–41

Chapter 4
Emotional Control and Anger Management

Lesson Outline
Guided Visualizations and Anger Monster Poster

Materials: newsprint, markers of various colors (or crayons), masking tape

1. Lead the class in an anger memory exercise. Step 1, Pages 46–47

2. Ask students what they experienced in their body when they were remembering a situation that made them angry. Step 2, Page 47

3. Conduct a calming visualization. Step 3, Page 47

4. Spread out newsprint to create an 'Anger Monster.' Step 4, Page 48

5. Create an outline of a student. Step 4, Page 48

6. Ask the students where in their body they felt physical changes when they were experiencing anger in the visualization. Draw and write their responses on the newsprint. Step 4, Page 49

7. Roll up the poster and have students return to their seats. Step 5, Page 50

8. Display the poster. Step 5, Page 50

9. Discuss and demonstrate how a person who does not maintain self-control when angry can turn into an anger monster. Step 5, Page 50

10. Have each student, on cue, become an emotional statue that expresses how they look when they are angry. Ask the students to be aware of the cues that indicate their body is experiencing anger. Step 6, Page 50

11. Finish this exercise with emotional statues of "relaxed" and "happy." Step 6, Page 50

Lesson Outline
Feeling Clouds and Charades

Materials per person: 8½ × 11 paper, pencil

1. Explain that each individual has to learn how to recognize their anger and other emotions and still maintain calm, rational behavior. Step 1, Pages 51–52

2. Explain that calming strategies include taking slow, deep breaths, taking a walk, writing in a journal, listening to soft music, going for a run, exercising, playing the drums, or throwing a ball. Step 1, Pages 51–52

3. Instruct the students in making a 'Feeling Cloud.' Step 2, Page 52

4. Have students write down three calming strategies that would work for them. Step 3, Page 53

5. Explain the Charades game. Step 4, Pages 53–54

6. Demonstrate how Charades is played by showing an example of a calming technique. Step 4, Pages 53–54

7. Have the class play Charades using self-calming choices. Step 5, Page 54

Lesson Extension: Mood music, Pages 54–55

Lesson Outline
Deep Breathing and Positive Affirmations

Materials: none

1. Explain the value of deep breathing and positive affirmations. Step 1, Page 56

2. Demonstrate the proper technique of deep breathing and positive affirmations. Step 2, Page 56

3. Demonstrate improper techniques of deep breathing. Step 3, Pages 56–57

4. Lead the class in deep breathing. Step 4, Page 57

5. Add affirmations to the deep breathing exercise. Step 5, Pages 57–58

Lesson Extension: Jumping Jacks, Page 58

Lesson Outline
ABCD Exercise

Materials: none

1. Write the letters "A," "B," "C," and "D" on the board vertically. Step 2, Pages 59–60

2. One by one, write out and discuss what word each letter represents. Step 2, Pages 59–60

3. Teach the physical reminders of the ABCD exercise. Step 2, Pages 59–60

4. Demonstrate the ABCD exercise and the physical reminders. Step 3, Page 60

5. Practice the exercise with the students. Step 4, Pages 60–61

6. When proficient, instruct the students to add, "walk away" to Step C and Step D. Practice the exercise. Step 5, Page 61

7. Conclude the ABCD exercise with deep breathing and positive affirmations as Steps C and D. Step 6, Pages 61–62

Chapter 5
Teaching Assertiveness

Lesson Outline
Teaching Assertive Communication

Materials per student: paper, pencil

1. Explain the advantages of assertive communication. Step 1, Page 64

2. Teach the details of each of the qualities of assertive communication. Step 2, Pages 65–70

3. Discuss and demonstrate the other styles of communication: aggressive, passive, and passive-aggressive. Step 3, Pages 70–72

Lesson Outline
Handshaking

Materials: none

1. Explain that a proper handshake is a good way to understand how to communicate assertively. Page 72

2. Discuss and demonstrate a proper handshake. Steps 1 and 2, Pages 73–74

3. Discuss and demonstrate improper handshakes: aggressive (including twisting), passive, palm pinch, and passive-aggressive. Step 3, Pages 74–77

4. Have the students practice proper handshaking with each other. Step 4, Page 77

5. Practice shaking hands with students. Step 5, Page 77–78

Lesson Outline
Recognizing Assertive, Aggressive, and Passive Communication Styles

Materials: three large pieces of paper; one with the word AGGRESSIVE written on it, one with ASSERTIVE on it, one with PASSIVE on it; tape

1. Create a space for the students to move around. Step 1, Pages 79–80

2. Divide the room into three sections: passive, assertive, and aggressive (assertive section between passive and aggressive). Step 1, Pages 79–80

3. Explain the instruction of the activity. Step 2, Page 80

4. Read and role-play the first scenario. Step 3, Pages 80–81

5. Say, "Go," to have the students determine if the communication style presented was passive, assertive, or aggressive. Step 3, Pages 80–81

6. Ask students how they determined which communication style was used. Step 3, Pages 80–81

Lesson Outline
Practicing Assertive Statements

Materials: paper or index cards with assertive statements on them (see Resource B)

1. Remind the students of the five qualities of assertive communication. Step 1, Page 82

2. Explain that each student will make a statement assertively, using prepared statements. Step 2, Page 82

3. Hand out one assertive statement card to each student. Step 2, Page 82

4. Have each student address you and read their statement. Step 2, Page 82

Lesson Extension: Ask the student, *"When would you have to make a statement like this?"* Page 83

Lesson Extension: Have students compare how to make the statements aggressively and passively. Page 83

Lesson Outline
Assertiveness Role-Plays

Materials: scenarios cards (see Resource C)

1. Put two chairs in front of the room to represent a stage. Step 1, Page 85

2. Tell the students that they will be role-playing situations that call for an assertive response. You will be the person to whom they are speaking. Steps 1 and 2, Pages 85–86

3. Hand out the role-playing scenario cards. Give the students a few minutes to consider how they would respond if they were really in the situation. Step 3, Page 86

4. Role-play with the students. Step 4, Pages 86–87

Chapter 6
Responding to a Bully

Lesson Outline
Bully Proofing Plan of Action

Materials: paper (per student), pencil (per student), adult

1. Tell the students that they will learn how to respond to someone who is *directly* bullying them. Step 1, Page 90

2. Review the definition of bully and different types of bullying with the students. Step 2, Pages 90–91

3. On the board write "Bully Proofing Plan of Action." Toward the bottom of the board, write, "Severity Clause: Protect your body at all times." Step 3, Pages 91–92

4. Discuss the severity clause. Step 3, Pages 91–92

5. Under the words Bully Proofing Plan of Action, write, "Ignore and/or walk away." Discuss and demonstrate how to ignore and/or walk away from a bully. Step 4 and Step 5, Pages 92–96

6. Add to the list, "Assertively say 'Stop!' *and* walk away." Discuss and demonstrate how to walk away from an aggressor. Step 6, Pages 96–100.

7. Add to the list, "Go to a trusted adult." Discuss how to talk to an adult about the problem. Step 7, Pages 100–101

Lesson Outline
Role-Playing the Bully Proofing Plan of Action

Materials: none

1. Ask for a volunteer to role-play the Bullying Proofing Plan of Action. Step 1, Pages 102–103

2. Role-play various scenarios with students. Step 1, Pages 102–103

3. Have the students practice the Bully Proofing Plan of Action with each other. Step 2, Pages 103–104

Chapter 7
The Power of Bystanders

Lesson Outline
What's A Bystander To Do?

Materials per student: paper, pencil

1. Discuss the term, and influence of, bystanders. Step 1, Page 111

2. Write: "What's A Bystander to Do?" Below that, write: "Don't join in—remove yourself." Step 2, Pages 111–112

3. To the list, add, "Tell the bullying person to 'Stop.'" Discuss and demonstrate. Step 3, Pages 112–114

4. Add to the list, "Separate the bullying student away from the person being bullied." Discuss and demonstrate. Step 4, Pages 114–115

5. Add to the list, "Separate the person being bullied away from the bully(s)." Discuss and demonstrate. Step 5, Pages 115–116

6. To the list on the board, add, "Report to a trusted adult." Step 6, Pages 116–117

7. Discuss Tattling vs. Telling. Step 7, Pages 117–119

8. Create groups of three or four students. Step 8, Pages 119–120

9. Provide bullying scenarios. Have students discuss how they might respond if they were a bystander in each of the bullying scenarios. Step 9, Pages 120–121

10. Provide Tattling vs. Telling scenarios. Have students discuss if choosing to talk to an adult about a situation would be tattling or telling. Step 10, Pages 121–122

Chapter 8
Playful Teasing vs. Hurtful Taunting

Lesson Outline
Defining Playful Teasing vs. Hurtful Taunting

Materials per student: paper, pencil

1. On the board, write:
   - "Lighten up. You're too sensitive."
   - "I was just kidding."
   - "I'm just teasing you."
   - "I didn't mean anything by it."
   - "Can't you take a joke?"
   Step 1, Page 126

2. Explain the differences between playful teasing and hurtful taunting. Step 2, Pages 126–128

3. Discuss with the class sensitive issues to consider before attempting to playfully tease. Step 2, Pages 126–128

4. Create groups of three or four students. Step 3, Page 128

5. You Be The Judge: present to the groups the Playful Teasing or Hurtful Taunting scenarios. Step 3, Pages 129–131

6. Have each group determine if the described scenario was teasing or taunting. Step 3, Pages 129–131

7. Have the students explain what criteria they used to determine if the scenario described was teasing or taunting. Step 3, Pages 129–131

   Lesson Extension: Don't Ever Tease About . . ., Page 131

   Lesson Extension: Bullying or Play Fighting, Page 132

   Lesson Extension: Flirting or Sexual Harassment, Page 132

Chapter 9
Making Friends: Strategies to Resist Social Aggression

Lesson Outline
Likes and Yikes—Determining Friendship Qualities

Materials per group: an 8½ × 11 paper, pencil

1. On the board write, "I have a mean friend." Discuss the meaning of this statement. Step 1, Page 137

2. Ask students what qualities they want in a friend. Write three responses on the board. Step 1, Page 137

3. Divide the class into groups of four to six students. In each group assign a scribe. Step 2, Page 137

4. Have each group brainstorm eight to twelve qualities they want in a friend. Have the scribe write down these qualities. Step 2, Page 137

5. Instruct each individual in the group to put a check mark next to the top three qualities they most value. Have each group circle the qualities with the most votes. Step 3, Pages 137–138

6. Draw a circle on the board. Inside the circle draw a person with a happy face. Step 4, Page 138

7. Within the circle, write down the most popular responses from each group. Step 5, Pages 138–139

8. Have each group brainstorm qualities they *will not* accept in a friendship. Instruct each individual to put a check mark next to three qualities they believe are the worst qualities. Have each group circle the qualities with the most votes. Step 6, Page 140

9. Outside the circle, write down the qualities with the most votes from each group. Step 6, Page 140

10. Ask, *"If you want friends with the qualities you have listed inside the circle, what kind of qualities do you have to have?"* Step 7, Pages 140–141

11. Post a copy of the Likes and Yikes results where students line up. Step 8, Page 141

Lesson Outline
Personal Boundaries

Materials: three bandanas or colored index cards: one green, one yellow, one red
Do not let the students know that you have the bandanas or index cards.

1. Create a space in the room. Step 1, Page 142

2. Choose a student volunteer (Vonnie) who is aware of and enforces their personal boundaries. With this student, choose three other students for the activity. Have students and yourself surround Vonnie. Step 2, Pages 142–143

3. One by one, call names of each student to walk towards Vonnie until Vonnie says, "Stop." Step 3, Page 143

4. Point out the difference between how close each person was allowed to get to Vonnie. Step 4, Pages 143–144

5. Discuss how a person determines their personal boundaries. Step 5, Page 144

6. Choose another student volunteer (Vonnie). Step 6, Page 144

7. Stand 15 feet from Vonnie. Walk slowly until Vonnie says, "Stop." Display green bandana. Step 7, Pages 144–145

8. Stand 15 feet from Vonnie. Walk slowly until Vonnie says, "Stop," but keep walking. Realize that you crossed the boundary, step back, and apologize. Display yellow bandana. Step 8, Page 145

9. Stand 15 feet from Vonnie. Walk slowly towards Vonnie. Continue even when Vonnie says, "Stop." Finally stop and display red bandana. Step 9, Page 145

10. Clarify the importance of respecting both physical and emotional boundaries. Step 9, Page 145

Lesson Outline
Finding New Friends

Materials: one copy of the Personal Interest Inventory for each student (see Page 149), pencil for each student

1. Ask the students to remind you of the qualities they desire in a friendship. Step 1, Page 147

2. Have students fill in the Personal Interest Inventory sheet. Step 2, Page 147

3. Give some examples of what might be on some students' papers. Have students stand if they have written the example on their paper. Step 3, Pages 147–149

4. Tell students that the information from the Personal Interest Inventory will provide clues as to who in the class has similar interests and who might make good prospective friends. Step 3, Pages 147–149

References

Aldrich, L. M. (2001). *Bullying: the affect and effect of bullying and being bullied.* Cherry Hill, NJ: M&K Publishing, Inc.

Austin, G., Huh-Kim, J., Skager, R., & Furlong, M. (2002, Winter). *2001–2002 California student survey.* Jointly sponsored by California Attorney General's Office, California Department of Education, and Department of Alcohol and Drug Programs. Published by California Attorney General's Office, Bill Lockyer, Attorney General.

Batsche, G. M., & Knoff, H. M. (1994). Bullies and their victims: Understanding a pervasive problem in the schools. *School Psychology Review, 23*(2), 165–174.

Bender, E. (2007). Teen researchers raise awareness about consequences of bullying. *Psychiatric News, 18*(42), 12.

Bullying Statistics (n.d.), Retrieved November 1, 2007, from http://www.atriumsoc.org/pages/bullyingstatistics.html

Chamberlain, S. P., Limber, S., & Cedillo, S. (2003). Responding to bullying. *Intervention in School and Clinic, 38*(4), 237–242.

Charach, A., Pepler, D., & Ziegler, S. (1995). Bullying at school—a Canadian perspective: A survey of problems and suggestions for intervention. *Education Canada, 35*(1), 12–18.

Crawford, N. (2002, October). New Ways to Stop Bullying. *American Psychological Association Monitor on Psychology, 33*(9).

Crick, N. R. & Grotpeter, J. K. (1995). Relational aggression, gender, and social psychological adjustment. *Child Development, 66*(3), 710–722.

Ericson, N. (2001, June). *Addressing the problem of juvenile bullying.* Office of Juvenile Justice and Delinquency Prevention, National Center for Conflict Resolution Education.

Gallo, C. (2007, February 13). It's not your mouth that speaks volumes. *Business Week.*

Garrett, A. G. (2003). *Bullying in American schools.* Jefferson, NC: McFarland.

Girl Scout Research Institute. (2003). *Feeling safe: What girls say.* New York, NY: Girl Scout Research Institute.

Grunbaum, J. A., Konn, L., Kinchen, S. A., Williams, B., Ross, J. G., Lowry, R., & Kolbe, L. (2002, October). National survey of students, gr. 5–12, 2001. Youth risk behavior surveillance, United States, 2001. *Journal of School Health, 72*(8), 313–328.

Hoover, J., Oliver, R., & Hazler, R. J. (1992). Bullying: Perceptions of adolescent victims in the Midwestern USA. *School Psychology International, 13*, 5–16.

Josephson Institute of Ethics. (2001). *2000 report card: Report #1, the ethics of American youth: Violence and substance abuse: Data & commentary.* Retrieved November 1, 2007, from http://www.josephsoninstitute.org/

Kaiser Family Foundation & Nickelodeon. (2001). *Talking with kids about tough issues: A national survey of parents and kids.* Menlow Park, CA: Kaiser Family Foundation.

Kendall-Tackett, K., & Giacomoni, S. (2005). *Child victimization: Maltreatment, bullying and dating violence, prevention and intervention.* New York, NY: Civic Research Institute, Inc.

Kohn, A. (1991). Caring Kids: The role of the schools. *Phi Delta Kappan, 72*(7), 496–506.

Lutgen-Sandvick, P., Tracy, S. J., & Alberts, J. K. (2007). Burned by bullying in the American workplace: Prevalence, perception, degree and impact. *Journal of Management Studies, 44*(6), 837–862.

Lyznicki, J. M., McCaffree, M. A., & Robinowitz, C. (2004). Safe school initiative. *American Family Physician,* 70: 1723–8, 1729–30.

Mayo Clinic. (2001). *Headline watch: One-third of U.S. kids affected by bullying.* Mayo Foundation for Medical Education and Research (MFMER).

Myers, R. (2001). *Lethal violence in schools.* Alfred, NY: Alfred University.

Nansel, T. R., Overpeck, M., Pilla, R. S., Ruan, W. J., Simons-Morton, B., & Scheidt, P. (2001). Bullying behaviors among U.S. youth: Prevalence and association with psychosocial adjustment. *Journal of the American Medical Association, 285*(16), 2094–2100.

National Crime Prevention Council. (2003). *Bullying, not terrorist attack, biggest threat seen by U.S. teens.* Washington, DC: National Crime Prevention Council.

National Institutes of Health. (2001). *Bullying widespread in U.S. schools survey finds.* Retrieved November 1, 2007, from http://www.nih.gov/news/pr/apr2001/nichd-24.htm

Nelson, M. F. (n.d.). *A qualitative study of effective school discipline practices: Perceptions of administrators, tenured teachers, and parents in twenty schools.* Retrieved December 31, 2007, from http://etd-submit.etsu.edu/etd/theses/available/etd-1106102-134400/unrestricted/NelsonF111202a.pdf

Oliver, R., Hoover, J. H., & Hazler, R. (1994). The perceived roles of bullying in small-town Midwestern schools. *Journal of Counseling and Development, 72*(4), 416–419.

Olweus, D. (1978). *Aggression in the schools: Bullies and whipping boys.* Washington, DC: Hemisphere.

Olweus, D. (1993). *Bullying at school.* Cambridge, MA: Blackwell.

Olweus, D., Limber, S., & Mihalic, S. (1999). *Blueprints for violence prevention, book nine: Bullying prevention program.* Boulder, CO: Center for the Study and Prevention of Violence.

Puhl, R., & Latner, J. (2007). Obesity, stigma, and the health of the nation's children. *Psychological Bulletin, 133*(4), 557–580.

Rigby, K. & Johnson, B. (n.d.) *Bystander behaviour of South Australian schoolchildren observing bullying and sexual coercion.* Retrieved December 31, 2007, from http://www.unisa.edu.au/hawkeinstitute/hpw/documents/rigby-bystander.doc

Saarni, C. (1999). *The development of emotional competence.* New York: The Guilford Press.

Sarazen, J. (2002). *Bullies and their victims: Identification and interventions.* Retrieved December 31, 2007, from http://www.uwstout.edu/lib/thesis/2002/2002sarazenj.pdf

Schwartz, J. (2006, September 12). *Violence in the home leads to higher rates of childhood bullying.* UPI, via ClariNet. *University of Washington News.* Retrieved November 1, 2008, from http://uwnews.org/article.asp?articleid=26586

Shaw, M. (2001). *Promoting safety in schools: International experience and action.* Monograph prepared for The United States Department of Justice, Bureau of Justice Assistance.

Shaw, M. (2003). Bullying: A comprehensive approach to prevention. *Inside School Safety, 8*(2), 2–4.

Weinhold, B. K., & Weinhold, J. B. (1998). Conflict resolution: The partnership way in schools. *Counseling and Human Development, 30*(7), 1–2.

HOW TO STOP BULLYING AND SOCIAL AGGRESSION